Blunders in International Business

This book is dedicated to those whose blunders
made the book possible

Blunders in International Business

Fourth Edition

David A. Ricks
University of Missouri, St Louis

Blackwell Publishing

© 1974, 1993, 1999, 2006 by David A. Ricks

BLACKWELL PUBLISHING
350 Main Street, Malden, MA 02148-5020, USA
9600 Garsington Road, Oxford OX4 2DQ, UK
550 Swanston Street, Carlton, Victoria 3053, Australia

The right of David A. Ricks to be identified as the Author of this Work has been asserted in accordance with the UK Copyright, Designs, and Patents Act 1988.

First edition published 1974 as *International Business Blunders* by Grid, Inc.
Second edition published 1993 by Blackwell Publishers Ltd
Third edition published 1999 by Blackwell Publishers Ltd
Fourth edition published 2006 by Blackwell Publishing Ltd

5   2008

Library of Congress Cataloging-in-Publication Data

Ricks, David A.
    Blunders in international business / David A. Ricks. — 4th ed.
        p. cm.
    Includes bibliographical references and index.
    ISBN-13: 978-1-4051-3492-7 (pbk. : alk. paper)   1. International business enterprises—Management—Case studies. 2. Business failures—Case studies. I. Title.

HD62 .4 .R53   2006
658'.049—dc22   2005057059

A catalogue record for this title is available from the British Library.

Set in 11.5/13.5pt Garamond
by Graphicraft Limited, Hong Kong
Printed and bound in the United Kingdom
by TJ International, Padstow, Cornwall

The publisher's policy is to use permanent paper from mills that operate a sustainable forestry policy, and which has been manufactured from pulp processed using acid-free and elementary chlorine-free practices. Furthermore, the publisher ensures that the text paper and cover board used have met acceptable environmental accreditation standards.

For further information on
Blackwell Publishing, visit our website:
www.blackwellpublishing.com

Contents

Preface

We often hear of business success stories. It seems that everyone is willing to relate past successes. However, unless these tales are absolutely incredible, we tend to forget them and consequently learn little of value.

Mistakes, on the other hand, are seldom admitted, are easily remembered, and can be used to illustrate valuable lessons. In fact, I began this collection of international business blunders when I discovered how effectively they could be used in the classroom. One day, after discussing what many of my students thought was a minor point related to international business, I cited a few blunders made by firms that had overlooked the concepts under discussion. The students thoroughly enjoyed the blunders—so much so that not only did they remember the concepts but they also wanted to learn more about international business.

As I encountered more reported blunders, I incorporated them into my classroom lectures with similar results and began to realize that I had stumbled on to a useful and enjoyable teaching tool. At this point, I decided to search seriously for blunders committed by multinational corporations. With the assistance of Professor Jeffrey S. Arpan, University of South Carolina; Marilyn Y.C. Fu Harpster, a former Ohio State graduate student; and Professor Donald Patton, Dalhousie

University, I corresponded with those teaching international business and scoured the journals and business periodicals searching for blunders. We published a few articles, and in 1974 wrote a book called *International Business Blunders*, which was published by Grid, Inc.

The book was favorably reviewed in *Business Week* and *Forbes*, and was also well received within the academic community. As I continued to gather reports of new or different blunders, the collection grew and gained the attention of the news media. As the public became aware of my collection, individuals began sending me evidence of even more blunders. All of this eventually led to suggestions that I write about the cases in multinational marketing I had uncovered.

I did so and the book, *Big Business Blunders: Mistakes in Multinational Marketing*, was published in 1983 by Richard D. Irwin, Inc. The book sold well to both the trade and the academic communities. However, it did not contain many of the nonmarketing blunders I had uncovered.

In order to include a wider variety of international business blunders, I wrote *Blunders in International Business*. It was published by Blackwell in 1993.

Since then I have learned of even more blunders that have occurred in all areas of international business. I now welcome the opportunity to share my latest updated collection with you because I truly believe that we can learn from the mistakes of others. Of course, it is not the only learning method, but it is an interesting and enjoyable one and surely preferable to learning through experience.

Many individuals have aided me in the collection and presentation of these blunders. My former co-authors— Jeffrey S. Arpan, Marilyn Harpster, Donald Patton, and Vijay Mahajan—were tremendous in their encouragement and assistance in previous research efforts. I especially appreciate their understanding and tolerance of my continuing interest in these blunders. Lesley Williams was an invaluable editor of two earlier editions. Karen Gruess-Steinman and Aysin Koparan, former students at the University of Missouri–St Louis; Linda Norwicz and Kari Morgenthaler, former students at Thunderbird, The American Graduate School of International Management; Peter Bemelman, Katherine Huelster, Martin Meznar, and Pedro Sanabria, former graduate students in international business at the University of South Carolina; and former Ohio State University student Jeff Sugheir have aided by serving as research assistants. Several other people have been of assistance by sending me information about business blunders. To all these people, I wish to express my sincere appreciation.

David A. Ricks

CHAPTER 1

Introduction

- The Role of Culture
- The Role of Communication
- Structure

CHAPTER 1

Introduction

Learn from the mistakes of others. You can't live long enough to make them all yourself.

Anonymous

The only constant in international business is change. Accompanying change is the possibility of unexpected events. Fortunately, some of these surprising occurrences prove to be advantageous to the multinational companies involved. For example, a U.S. firm selling feminine sanitary napkins in South America suddenly experienced a major surge in sales. The company was delighted, although a bit startled, when it discovered that the sales boost was prompted by local farmers buying the napkins to use as dust masks! No less surprised was a U.S. company which sold toothbrushes in South Vietnam during the late 1960s. It too experienced an unexpected increase in sales. Years later the company learned why—the Vietcong had purchased the toothbrushes to use for weapon cleaning.

Other firms have also encountered unexpected product marketability as a result of unplanned and often unimagined uses for their products. These surprises, although sometimes controversial, are normally welcomed by the "lucky" companies. For example, an unimagined use of a product occurred during the Persian Gulf War when news spread that the U.S. troops were using condoms to protect rifle barrels from sand. As a result the condom company's stock skyrocketed. However, not all firms experience such good fortune. In fact, many surprises in international business are quite undesirable.

Sometimes companies are caught off guard by an unavoidable turn of events. Other times, though, they are unhappily surprised by outcomes that they could have avoided. A company is said to have "blundered" if it makes a decision resulting in a costly or embarrassing situation that was foreseeable and avoidable.

The foreign environment has been especially difficult for some to analyze. Many mistakes, for example, have been made because managers have failed to remember that consumers differ from country to country. Buyers, influenced by local economic constraints and by local values, attitudes, and tastes, differ in what they buy, why they buy, how they buy, when they buy, and where they buy. Managers who have failed to recognize these differences have committed a number of blunders.

The Role of Culture

Cultural differences are the most significant and troublesome variables encountered by the multinational company. The failure of managers to comprehend fully these disparities has led to most international business blunders. A European businessman, for example, while on an important negotiating trip to China, playfully flipped a piece of ice from his drink towards his companion. Unluckily for him, the ice accidentally landed on a nearby official and the businessman was soon sent packing. Another unlucky individual found himself home sooner than expected after he flippantly patted a waitress. The Chinese simply do not accept such foolishness—as many a playful visitor can attest.

Without fully understanding the local culture, trying to "do as the Romans do" can be a dangerous thing.

A former president of American Express, Japan, for example, learned this the hard way. On New Year's Day 1985, he was featured in a full-page ad in a photo of himself wearing a Japanese kimono. Apparently, no foreigner had done this before and it was suspected by many Japanese that it was intended as a joke to make fun of the local culture. Some even complained that it was an intentional attempt to humiliate the Japanese.

In 1983 Columbia Pictures produced a four-hour movie set in Egypt that resulted in the banning of all Columbia films in Egypt. The Egyptian authorities were offended by the numerous inaccuracies that included accent (Pakistani), clothing (Moroccan), and behavior (American). Nasser, for example, was portrayed publicly kissing his wife—an unacceptable act in Egypt and in many other countries.

Cultural differences often show up during ceremonies, such as in the case of a Toronto Blue Jays baseball game. The U.S. Marine color guard made the mistake of displaying the Canadian flag turned upside down, with the top of the red maple leaf pointed downward. As the scene was displayed on Canadian television, the Canadian switchboards lit up and Toronto news-papers were filled with viewer reactions to the obvi-ous error.

During the groundbreaking ceremonies for Hitachi Ltd's subsidiary, Hitachi Automotive Products (USA), Inc., the Governor of Kentucky presented the Japanese executives with a flag of the Commonwealth of Kentucky. After opening the flag for all to see, the Japanese care-lessly dragged it along the ground. In Japan (and in many other countries), flags are not treated with the same respect as they are in America. The Japanese really meant no disrespect; they simply were unaware of U.S. customs about flags. However, many in the audience, especially the older Americans, were offended.

We all know that some things are done differently by the people of other countries, but sometimes these differences are hard to embrace. Consider, for instance, what happened when a man from Tonga answered a neighbor's ad in the Salt Lake City newspaper. The neighbor wanted to sell his son's pony. When the neighbor asked the Tongan why he wanted to purchase the pony, the Tongan replied that he wanted it for his own son's birthday. The seller was satisfied with the reply so the deal was closed. Then before the seller's eyes, the Tongan casually turned, picked up a board, and clubbed the pony to death. The dead pony was tossed into the Tongan's truck and hauled home. When the police arrived, they found a huge birthday party in progress with many Tongans happily cooking the pony for a typical Tongan birthday dinner.

All nationalities possess unique characteristics that must be understood. For example, Arabs typically dislike deadlines. An Arab faced with a deadline tends to feel threatened and backed into a corner. Many Americans, on the other hand, try to expedite matters by setting deadlines. Hundreds of U.S.-owned radio sets are sitting untouched in Middle Eastern repair shops because some Americans made the cultural mistake of requesting that the work be completed by a certain time.

U.S. business managers have encountered similar problems trying to understand time values in other cultures. One U.S. company lost a major contract opportunity in Greece because its managers tried to impose U.S. customs on the Greek negotiators. Besides being too forthright and outspoken in the eyes of the Greeks, the Americans tried to set time limits for the meetings. The Greeks, however, considered time limits insulting and thus felt that the Americans showed a lack of finesse. The Americans also wanted the Greeks to first agree to principles and then allow their subordinates to work out all necessary details. The Greeks viewed this as a deceptive strategy; they preferred to directly handle all arrangements regardless of the time involved.[1]

Protocol with regard to location is often the source of international blunders between cultures. A Chicago company was bidding on a public works project in Thailand and was waiting for the Thai contingent to arrive at their Chicago offices for the meeting. After hours of waiting, the Chicago company found out that the Thai group was still waiting to be picked up at the airport. They rescheduled a meeting for the next day, only to find out that the same communication problem existed. The Thai group waited for the Chicago company to pick them up at the hotel, while the Chicago company expected the Thai group to meet them at the Chicago office.

In France, McDonald's overlooked a cultural difference that led to years of litigation. In selecting a French partner, McDonald's examined a number of characteristics that would ensure sales. McDonald's is very good at this and, as usual, was successful. However, it did not examine carefully enough its partner's attitudes about cleanliness. Because French firms sometimes place less emphasis on cleanliness than U.S. firms do, local references of the French partner did not expose this as a troublesome issue. As business in France grew, however, McDonald's soon observed hygiene habits it considered unacceptable in its U.S. outlets. These habits, though, were not viewed as negatively by the French partner or by most of the French customers, for that matter. The real problem? Many of the outlet's customers were U.S. tourists expecting U.S. standards. The French outlets, therefore, negatively impacted McDonald's global image and threatened its "clean" reputation at home.

A local supermarket hoping to impress Japanese visitors served sushi and tea to its guests. Unfortunately, it not only served the fish cooked when the fish should have been served raw, but the supermarket also served *Chinese* tea.

The failure to understand cultural differences can bear serious consequences. Consider an unfortunate U.S. manager who worked in the South Pacific. He hired local people without considering the island's traditional status system. By hiring too many of one group, he threatened to alter the balance of power of the people. The islanders discussed this unacceptable situation and independently developed an alternative plan. It had taken them until 3 a.m. to do so, however. But since time was not important in their culture, they saw no reason to wait until morning to present their suggestions to the American. They casually went to his place of residence, but their arrival at such a late hour caused him to panic. Since he could not understand their language and could not imagine that they would want to discuss business at 3 a.m., he assumed that they were coming to riot and called in the Marines! It was some time before the company was able to get back to "business as usual."

Knowing what to do is as important as knowing what not to do. In India, for instance, it is considered a violation of sacred hospitality mores to discuss business in the home or on social occasions. And if a business executive from India offers "come any time," it is an honest invitation, not just a polite expression as often used in the United States. The Indian is requesting a visit but is politely allowing the guest to arrange the time of the meeting. If no time is set, the Indian will assume that the invitation has been refused. The failure to understand this local custom has led to some serious misunderstandings.

Even the rejection of a cup of coffee can cause major problems. While a very profitable opportunity was being negotiated, one U.S. executive innocently made the mistake of refusing a Saudi Arabian's friendly offer to join him for a cup of coffee. Such a rejection is considered an affront in Saudi Arabia. Naturally, the Saudi became much less sociable, and the negotiation process was much less successful than it might have been.

Gift giving can also create troubles. Sometimes gifts are expected and the failure to supply them is seen as insulting. Other times, however, the mere offer of such a token is considered offensive. In the Middle East, for example, hosts are insulted if guests bring food or drink to their homes, because they believe that such gifts imply that they are not good hosts. (Liquor, of course, is an especially dangerous gift, as it is prohibited by the Islamic religion.) In many parts of Latin America, cutlery or handkerchiefs should not be given, because these gifts imply a cutting off of a relationship or the likelihood of a tearful event. And giving a clock to some-one in China is not a good idea, either. The Chinese word for clock sounds similar to their word for funeral.

In fact, even the way in which a gift is presented is important. In most parts of Asia gifts should be given privately to avoid embarrassing the Asians, but in the Middle East they need to be offered publicly in order to reduce the possible impression that bribery is being attempted.[2]

To avoid making blunders, a person must be able to discern the difference between what must be done, what must not be done, and what may or may not be done. For example, shoes must be removed before entering many of the religious buildings of the world, but the individuals doing so must not act as if they are of the religion if, in fact, they are not.

Complete knowledge and understanding of a foreign culture, however, is almost impossible to acquire. In fact, no general agreement even exists as to what "culture" is, but most experts do concur that it is a complex set of variables involving a group's beliefs and ways of living.

They also agree that an understanding of any foreign culture requires knowledge in a great many areas. Unfortunately, even a well-intended person can commit a blunder by overlooking just one seemingly unimportant aspect of a foreign culture.

The Role of Communication

As stated, culture plays an important role in international business. Of all of the aspects of culture, communication may be the most critical and certainly has been involved in numerous blunders. Good communication linkages must be established between a company and its customers, its suppliers, its employees, and its host governments. Poor communication networks can and have caused difficulties.

Technology offers new ways to commit blunders. Some of these blunders are simply due to not fully understanding the technology but sometimes the blunder happens because the normal ways to detect mistakes don't always work. Therefore new technology requires us to develop new ways to detect errors.

Take, for example, the use of the Internet to obtain data. More uses for the Internet are being developed daily, but not without some problems and challenges. Many textbooks now make more additional material that interfaces with their books available on the Internet. This material can be updated and provide valuable support for the learning experience. However, care must be taken to insure that the results are as anticipated.

Professors Michael Moffett and Arthur Stonehill, for example, had problems with the 1998 edition of their very good international financial management textbook when their readers were given an Internet address for checking their learning progress (answers to exercises, etc.). The problem was that the address given was just slightly incorrect. The address turned out to provide X-rated (not FX) material. (It might be noted, however, that authors of some of the other competing books wondered if this was really an accident.)

Because so many potential communication barriers exist, it is especially difficult for companies to effectively communicate with potential buyers. Messages can be translated incorrectly, inappropriate media used, regulations overlooked, and economic or taste differences ignored. Sometimes the potential customer never receives the company's message, and at other times the message arrives but because of its ineffectiveness is of little value. Every once in a while the buyer receives the message but, to the company's dismay, the message sent was incorrect.

For example, it certainly would not be wise to say "yeah" to the Japanese. Not wise, that is, unless one wants to say "no," because "yeah" sounds like the Japanese word for "no." However, saying "so" should cause no problems—it means the same in both languages. (In China, by the way, *boo-shih* means, "not true." Americans have a remarkably similar-sounding phrase they sometimes use when wanting to imply they don't believe something!)

Multinational companies are not the only entities vulnerable to communication problems, of course. Former President Carter's speech in Poland will long be remembered for his incorrectly translated appreciation of the Polish women (whom his translator said he "lusted for"). Other well-known people have mangled public introductions by using incorrect titles and names. It seems that if there is a way to say something incorrectly, some poor soul has managed to do so.

As was noted earlier, even Professors of International Business have been known to make mistakes. Indiana

University, for example, hosted an important international business conference in 2002 and invited five distinguished speakers to talk about the history of international business education. Dr. John Daniels, past president of the Academy of International Business and a highly visible researcher in the field of international business, was one of the special speakers. As he was about to make his presentation, however, he saw he had a problem. Sitting in the audience was a person whom Dr. Daniels had identified in his already circulated paper as dead.

Communication problems take many forms. Nonverbal communication difficulties, in particular, have led to serious blunders. Americans, for example, all too often forget the old proverb that "patience is a virtue." On many occasions, this lapse of memory has led them to react inappropriately by trying to correct a situation when in actuality all that was needed was patience. The "improper" amount of touching or eye contact has left many people feeling so uncomfortable that effective communication efforts have been hampered. The "incorrect" distance between individuals engaged in conversation has led to the false conclusion that the other person is too aggressive and hostile or too cold and distrustful.

The peoples of each culture uniquely utilize body movements as methods of communication. The meanings of motions and signs common in one culture may relay something quite different in another. Consider, for example, the OK sign commonly used in the United States. In France it signifies zero, and in Japan it symbolizes money. In parts of South America, however, it is a vulgar gesture. One unfortunate company learned this when it had an entire catalog printed with an OK stamp on each page. Although the error was quickly discovered, it created a costly six-month delay while all of the catalogs were reprinted.

Headshakes are particularly difficult to interpret. People in the United States shake their heads up and down to signify "yes." Many British, however, make the same motions just to indicate that they hear—not necessarily that they agree. To say "no," people shake their heads from side to side in the United States, jerk their heads back in a haughty manner in the Middle East, wave a hand in front of the face in the Orient, and shake a finger from side to side in Ethiopia.

Asian Indians sometimes shift their heads from side to side in a slightly jerky manner to indicate interest. However, in New Zealand people suck in a bit of air to show the same interest. The U.S. gesture to slit one's throat means "I love you" in Swaziland. A backward victory symbol is an insulting gesture in Europe. Using a palm-up hand with moving index finger connotes "come here" in many countries but is considered vulgar in others. In Ethiopia, one beckons another by holding out the hand, palm down, and repeatedly closing the hand. The act of folding one's arms denotes respect in Fiji but indicates arrogance in Finland. To an Ethiopian, one finger to the lips requests silence from a child whereas four fingers to the lips are necessary to ask the same from an adult.

The pointing of a finger is a dangerous action. In North America it is a very normal gesture, but it is considered very rude in many other parts of the world—especially in areas of Asia and Africa. It is usually much safer to merely close the hand and point with the thumb. However, even though pointing the thumb up is an easily recognized positive gesture in North America, that same thumbs-up signal is a vulgar insult in the Middle East.

Many cultures also have their own form of greeting. Often it is some variation of a handshake, but people also greet each other with hugs, nose rubs, kisses, and other gestures in other cultures. Failure to be aware of these customs has led to awkward and embarrassing encounters and to serious misunderstandings.

Other forms of communication have also caused problems. The tone of the voice, for example, can be important. Some cultures permit people to raise their voices when they are distant from one another, but loudness in other cultures is often associated with anger or a loss of self-control.

Even laughter is interpreted differently around the world. While most countries consider it an expression of joy, some cultures discourage it. In many West African countries, laughter indicates embarrassment, discomfort, or surprise.

Ignorance of such differences in verbal and non-verbal forms of communication has resulted in many a social and business blunder. Local people tend to be willing to overlook most of the mistakes tourists make; after all, they are just temporary visitors. Locals are much less tolerant of the errors of business people—especially those who represent firms trying to project an impression of permanent interest in the local economy. The consequences of erring, therefore, are much greater for businesses.

Structure

Some of the blunders that companies have committed while trying to engage in business in foreign countries are described and discussed in this book. Most of these blunders have been reported in the media, but only in small numbers at any one time and in no clear patterns. The gathering of hundreds of these reports provided an opportunity to group these blunders and to arrive at some universally applicable conclusions.

The blunders have been grouped into seven categories: production, names, marketing, translation, management, strategy, and "other." Production blunders—especially those related to building plants on inappropriate sites—have generally proven to be the most costly. Plant location and plant layout errors as well as mistakes involving products and packages are reported in the next chapter.

As pointed out in Chapter 3, inappropriate product and company names have caused company headaches. On occasion, a company has introduced an old, established name in a country that misunderstands it. In other instances, a firm has created a new name, only to later regret its decision. Sometimes harmless and amusing, these blunders have at other times proven insulting, embarrassing, and costly.

Marketing mistakes are described in Chapter 4. Communication problems, poor promotional strategies, and cultural differences have all played a part in the development of major marketing blunders. These types of errors are identified and discussed.

The largest number of blunders has been due to faulty translations. In fact, the number of translation errors is so vast that they are reported in a separate chapter, Chapter 5. Carelessness, unexpected additional meanings, and improper use of idioms have all contributed to translation blunders.

Managerial blunders were generally caused because people did not understand or were not aware of cultural differences. Some people simply are not culturally sensitive enough to successfully handle international assignments. Others may be sensitive but uninformed. A number of the management problems reported in Chapter 6 were caused by management's lack of knowledge concerning local labor practices. These misunderstandings have often led to the most confrontational of all the reported incidents.

Strategic blunders are usually the most complex. They are also among the most difficult to overcome. Problems arising from companies' entry modes, their establishment of various alliances, and their planning of supply arrangements are discussed in Chapter 7.

Multinational enterprises have also been involved in many other blunders. Chapter 8 details legal, financial, and market research blunders. These types of blunders are not as easy to uncover and rarely make headlines, but they can be just as costly. In fact, the chapter helps make it clear that a blunder can occur in any area of international business.

The final chapter explains what can be learned from all of the international business blunders reported in the book and provides some important, basic conclusions. Some final comments and observations are also outlined in Chapter 9.

Please note that this book was not written with the intent of poking fun at companies. Nor should anyone conclude that firms are constantly making foolish mistakes. Their overall record is good, but hopefully this book will help make the future record even better.

CHAPTER 2

Production

- Location/Layout
- Product
- Package
- Color
- Summary

Production

A great deal of attention has been focused recently on the service industries. They have certainly grown in importance so it is easy to overlook the significance of other industries—ones that actually produce physical products. The production of physical products, however, is a vital part of international business.

Companies which manufacture physical products encounter their own unique set of risks and make blunders that firms in the service industries avoid. These blunders can involve the location or layout of the production activity, the product, or its package.

Location/Layout

Many years ago, a well-known multinational fiber producer, Celanese, purchased a large tract of land containing eucalyptus trees in Sicily. It planned to build a pulp processing plant and then use the local trees as raw material. It was not until the plant was built and production was to begin that the company discovered that the local trees were too small, the supply was too limited, and the logs were unsuitable for use. The result: the firm was forced to import pulp at a cost so high the plant ended up losing over $55 million. This very expensive lesson occurred because the company tried to save a few dollars and minimize its costs by not sending a specialist to Sicily to check on the trees prior to purchase.

Ill-suited or inappropriate production sites have also left deep wounds in many other firms. One U.S. food processor built a pineapple cannery at the delta of a river in Mexico. Since the pineapple plantation was located upstream, the company planned to float the ripe fruit down to the cannery on barges. To its dismay, however, the firm soon discovered that at harvest time the river current was far too strong for barge traffic. Since no other feasible alternative method of transportation existed, the plant was closed. The new equipment was sold for a fraction of its original cost to a Mexican group that immediately relocated the cannery. This seemingly simple navigational oversight proved quite expensive to the firm.

The Hanna Mining Company experienced some logistical problems in Brazil. One of the basic strategies of the firm involved its ability to supply extract ore at increasing rates over time. Since a small-scale operation could not prove profitable, the company decided that by expanding every year it would become a profitable operation by the time the firm was able to export 2 million tons of ore. Few initial problems developed. The company, however, was unable to expand its operations as expected because local transportation facilities were inadequate. In this case, the firm's strategy failed because it had no way to transport the ore to market even though it maintained the capability to extract the required ore. (It should be noted that Hanna Mining reports that this was not a foreseeable problem, since the local railroad authorities failed to fulfill the contract's maximum delivery requirement.)

As another example, a French firm set up a timber mill in East Africa and was all set to open the mill when the French realized that usually there was not enough electrical power in the area to run the mill. Unfortunately, there may never be. The French had to dismantle this useless mill.

Sometimes it is not the plant location which is the problem, but the plant layout. An English pulp and paper company, for example, entered into a joint venture arrangement with another British firm, hoping to utilize the timber resources of British Columbia. They obtained a concession of enormous timberland acreage. The sawmill, however, was designed and set up by British engineers who were unfamiliar with the characteristics of British Colombian lumber. As a result, the mill was constructed with a setup which was not flexible enough to adjust to the numerous varieties and sizes of Canadian trees. Within three years the firms sold the mill at a substantial loss.

A large British shipment of U.S.-made textile machinery motors was returned because the British did not receive the motors that they thought they had ordered. Apparently, a right-handed motor in an English mill is considered to be a left-handed motor in the United States. Americans look at the production run from downstream and thus see the motor opposite to the British, who view things from the start of the production run.

Product

In developed countries, we often take for granted the vast array of products available for sale. In many countries, however, such product variety and selection do not exist. The assumption that the absence of a product from an economy automatically indicates a potentially good or profitable market has led a number of companies down a thorny path. More than one company has failed to consider that, even if the local consumers can afford the product, they may not really want it or may be interested in it only if it is substantially modified to fit their local tastes and preferences.

These modifications, known as adaptations, exist in two major forms: product and package. Product modification or the alteration of the physical product is occasionally required for the product to conform to local tastes or local conditions. Adaptation of the package is often necessary to attract the customer to the product or to maintain the product's integrity in a unique environment. Occasionally, a firm is forced to modify both the package and the product to create a suitable product for the new market.

Product adaptation

Apple Computer entered the Japanese market before IBM, but it failed to take advantage of its head start. Apple tried to sell its U.S. models in Japan without modifying them. No efforts were made to even translate the user's manual into Japanese. Only after IBM entered the market using a customized approach did Apple realize its mistakes. Now that the company has translated its manual and has made some other changes, it is doing much better.

Similarly, Procter & Gamble encountered problems with the Japanese diaper market. After years of research, the company uncovered the problem: Japanese parents change diapers far more frequently than Americans but do not usually have the storage space of U.S. homes. Thus, larger boxes of disposable diapers posed a storage problem for the average Japanese family. Once Procter & Gamble began producing thinner diapers sold in a smaller box, the popularity of the new diapers,

"Ultra" Pampers, spread like a baby's rash and now it is the leading brand in Japan.

The Campbell Soup Company discovered that product modification could be an easier road to travel than consumer education when it tried to market its condensed soups in Great Britain. The company had used market-testing methods to confirm a British interest in its soups and had also priced the soup to be competitive. But initial sales were low: a result of the failure of the British to understand that the Campbell's soup was indeed priced competitively. The British were accustomed to buying canned soup but not in the condensed form. Therefore, it appeared to them that they were buying half as much soup for the same amount of money. Campbell Soup was faced with two choices: it could try to hurriedly mass educate the British buying public or it could alter the product. It wisely chose to modify its product by adding water so that its soups would be like the soups already accepted and found on the grocery shelves.

General Foods experienced similar difficulties when it tried to sell its U.S.-style "Jell-O" in Great Britain. Although the package of Jell-O contained the normal powdered substance Americans expect, the British simply were not interested. In Great Britain, the jellied form of such a product is the normal one to buy. To a Briton, if it does not jiggle and look good, then it simply is not "proper." By quickly changing its product to conform to the British norm, General Foods averted a possible disaster.

The sale of cigarettes outside the home country has been quite exasperating for several companies. The common presumption that all peoples enjoy identical products has often proven erroneous; in fact, some form of product modification has usually been necessary to gain market success. The failure to make the needed alteration, even though possibly a slight one, can radically hurt sales. More than one firm, for example, has encountered difficulties trying to sell filter-tipped cigarettes in the less developed countries. Consumers of wealthier nations, more aware of the health risks of smoking, are quite willing to pay a bit more for filtered cigarettes. In poor countries where life expectancy is often fewer than 30 years, the threat of death from lung cancer is lessened. Even if aware of the risks, the local smoker can usually neither afford the extra cost of the filtered cigarettes nor become too concerned about developing lung cancer at an advanced age. Consequently, the market for filter cigarettes in these countries is typically sluggish. Often the only modification needed to increase sales is the removal of the filter and the accompanying reduction in price.

Some products may require more technical modification, however. Obviously, if the electrical current available in a potential market is different from the home country market, then electrical products require adaptation before introduction. Measurement systems vary between countries, and often components need to be modified to adhere to local standards. Product sizes must also be considered. A British firm, for example, experienced problems selling in Japan until it remodeled its product $1/16$ in. to conform to Japanese specifications. Such small differences can easily cause major headaches for manufacturers. Fortunately, most companies quickly learn of these local standards and conditions and seldom introduce a totally inappropriate product. A much more difficult task is the detection of the subtle technical differences and the needed modifications.

Star Manufacturing Company of Japan quickly realized that it had introduced a printer that didn't arouse U.S. interests. The printer that had sold well in Japan did poorly in the United States because Americans wanted better graphics. The printer was soon modified and sales picked up immediately.

A duplicating machine manufacturer ran into serious problems in one country when it assumed that the quality paper required for its machines would be available. The local government owned its own paper company and, unfortunately, the paper size and quality were not highly standardized. Thus, the imported machines could not accommodate the varying characteristics. Because of the government's pride in its paper facilities, however, it would not allow the importation of the paper required. The machines sat idle, and the company's market was quickly closed. The company should have learned of this problem prior to its market entry. It then could have requested permission to import the correct paper, or it could have modified its machines to accommodate the local paper. Had neither been possible, the firm would have known not to market its products in that country.

Similarly, Polaroid planned to introduce a slide copier as a central piece of its 1989 product line for both U.S. and European markets. Unfortunately, the engineers failed to realize that standard paper sizes vary. Therefore, the copier would not work using standard European paper. Hasty modifications were made, but not without extra costs.

Marketing its liquid detergents in Europe proved to be a challenge for Procter & Gamble as European washing machines dispense powdered detergents. Adapters to the machines were not a feasible option because each brand of machine required a different design. Procter & Gamble eventually came up with the solution: a plastic ball was supplied with each bottle of detergent. The "dosing ball" could be filled with detergent and placed in each load of laundry. Procter & Gamble now holds 50 percent of the liquid detergent market in Europe.

Refrigerator manufacturers from the Western nations initially encountered great difficulty in selling their products in Japan. The refrigerator motors were the major problem; they were simply too noisy for the typical Japanese home, which was often built with literally paper-thin walls. Sears is cited as one of the companies most successful in the sale of Western refrigerators in Japan. It achieved this status by designing a refrigerator specifically for use in the local conditions.

General Motors of Canada experienced major technical problems with one of its cars in Iraq. It shipped 13,500 Chevrolet "Malibu" automobiles there only to discover that the cars were mechanically unfit for the hot and dusty climate. Iraq refused delivery of the remaining 12,000 autos, which had been ordered, until GM modified the vehicles so that they performed more reliably. GM tripled its number of engineers and mechanics in Baghdad, but by the time the company figured out that supplementary air filters and different clutches would eliminate the mechanical failures, it began to encounter political problems. Thus 12,000 automobiles specially designed for desert driving collected snow in Canada while GM waited for the political dust to settle.

Unexpected major adjustments also had to be made by a U.S. tire producer after it opened a plant in France. Based on its previous success in France, the tire manufacturer built a new production facility without conducting any market research. Because of the changing driving habits of the French, however, new kinds of tires were required and adjustments were forced upon the manufacturer. The company learned its lesson, of course. It hired a market research executive before building its next plant.

The necessity for product adaptation has existed for hundreds of years. England's East India Company possibly lost control of India in 1857 because it failed to modify a product it provided. In those days bullets were often encased in pig wax, and the tops had to be bitten off before the bullets could be fired. The Asian Indian soldiers were furious when they discovered the pig wax, since it was against their religion to eat pork. The soldiers revolted and hundreds were killed on both sides before peace was restored. The bullets were modified, but the East India Company lost control of India to the British Crown.[1]

Improper product modification can also lead to misery. China discovered this when it shipped shoes to Egypt. It had tried to make the shoes more appealing to the Egyptians by placing Arabic characters on the soles of the shoes. Unfortunately, the designers did not know Arabic and merely copied words from other material. The words they chose meant "God." It required China's ambassador to Egypt to soften the tension that resulted from this mistake.

Sometimes the modified product inadvertently reaches the wrong market. This too can cause problems. For example, one company received a great deal of unwanted attention from U.S. parents who purchased a talking doll they believed said, "Kill Mommy." These dolls, made in Hong Kong but shipped from Japan to many parts of the world, carried messages in the language of the country of destination. A packing error, however, caused some Spanish-speaking dolls to be sent to the United States. The Spanish message was "Quiero Mommy," which means "I love Mommy," but the rather poor-quality sound reproduction and the language difference altered the message and caused a media sensation.

Taste/Style

One variable often requiring modification is taste. Both the food and tobacco industries can attest to this. Philip

Morris encountered well-publicized problems when it tried to sell its U.S. blends in Canada. Many other companies have experienced similar difficulties in other countries. Most cigarette firms believe that "it is better to switch than fight," and cigarettes are now generally blended in deference to local taste preferences.

Vast numbers of food products have required taste adaptations in order to appeal to local consumers. General Foods experienced some problems and had to alter some of its coffees and foods to attract European and Japanese palates. Campbell Soup Company also was forced to change the flavor of some of its soups (notably the tomato soup) to suit European preferences. Many soft drinks have been modified to gain market acceptance in various parts of the world. Often all that is necessary is a subtle change, but without such variation, sales may slump. Both General Foods and Campbell Soup Company have enjoyed overseas successes because they realized this and acted accordingly. Nestlé has also successfully introduced dozens of blends of its Nescafé around the world.

Fast food chains have been especially quick to modify their offerings. McDonald's, for example, adjusts its menu for each foreign market. It has sold beer in Germany, wine in France, mutton pot pies in Australia, and "McSpaghetti" in the Philippines. Burger King in Venezuela does not use sesame seed buns, the milkshakes there are sweeter and creamier, and even the ketchup is much sweeter. Wendy's serves shrimp cake sandwiches in Japan. Shakey's sells chorizo in Mexico and squid in Japan. Arby's dropped its ham sandwiches from its menus in the Middle East. Kentucky Fried Chicken (KFC) serves "chips" rather than "fries" in England and has added rice and smoked chicken to its menus in Japan. KFC also initiated one of the more unique product modifications: in order to sell its chicken in Israel, it introduced kosher chicken.

"Pop-Tarts," which had proved to be quite a successful product in the United States, were unpopular in Britain. Not only was the taste considered too sweet there, but also most potential buyers at the time did not own toasters which could correctly warm the product. U.S. companies are not the only ones that have found that local tastes differ from those at home. European soups, for example, are considered too salty by most Americans and have not fared well on U.S. grocery shelves.

Food and tobacco manufacturers have not borne the effects of consumer preference alone. Style is another important ingredient in the product mix, and failure to reflect local style choices is also likely to cause financial losses for a company. Ford experienced well-publicized problems in Europe during the 1960s partially as a result of the amount of "Americanization" being introduced into the look of its European cars. Earlier style lines of Ford's European cars sold well in Europe because of their simple sleekness that was favored by the local people. When the more traditional aspects of the U.S. automobile (i.e., wideness, heaviness, and length) were incorporated into models of the 1960s, sales slumped. The sales resistance came to a halt when the cars produced once again reflected European tastes.

Cluett Peabody may have had similar problems, as its Belgian factory was closed after only three years. Cluett blames high costs for the closing, but Belgian retailers claim it was really due to a complaisant Belgian management which assented to U.S. styling, pricing, and sizing that were not in harmony with European tastes and budgets. Either cause for failure could have been eliminated through appropriate preliminary research and implementation of the indicated modifications.

Package

In many markets, the product may be quite acceptable but still may not sell well if housed in an inappropriate package. Packages play two key roles in marketing—they promote the product and they protect it. Packages that require long-distance shipping must be capable of withstanding the journey. Many companies have endeavored to export their products only to witness the return of crushed and partially empty containers. Others have tried to ship perishable goods by means requiring months for delivery. Still others have placed the goods in packages unable to withstand moisture (or other unique conditions). In one such case, a firm in Taiwan shipped some drinking glasses to the Middle East. The company used wooden crates and padded the glasses with hay. Most of the glasses, however, were broken by the time they reached their destination. As the crates traveled into the drier Middle East, the moisture content of the hay dropped, and by the time the crates were delivered, the thin straw offered almost no protection. What works well in one part of the world doesn't necessarily work well everywhere!

Another Taiwanese firm encountered a similar problem. The Iranians refused payment on a shipment of wool because they claimed that the shipper lied about the weight of the shipment. After expensive delays, it was discovered that wool originating in humid countries (such as Taiwan) loses moisture when shipped to dry countries (such as Iran), and therefore weighs less after being shipped!

In some climates, packages must be specially designed to assure product survival. Quaker Oats, for example, uses special vacuum-sealed tins to protect its products sold in hot and humid countries.

Local storage conditions also vary, and the package must be an appropriate size and shape. Coca-Cola tried to introduce the two-liter plastic bottle in Spain, but market entry was difficult. The company soon discovered that few Spaniards had refrigerator doors with compartments large enough to accommodate the large-size bottle.

Detergents must be packaged differently to sell well in different countries. Americans, for example, are less concerned than Germans with such details as chemical actions and how the detergent actually works. The German package, therefore, must be modified to contain this extra information.

Seemingly harmless package labels have sometimes proven to be embarrassing to the company or even insulting to its potential consumers. One soft drink company inadvertently offended some of its customers in the Arab world because its labels incorporated six pointed stars. The stars were only considered to be a decoration by the firm, but the Arabs interpreted them as reflecting pro-Israeli sentiments. Naturally, the label had to be altered. Another company printed the label on its product in ten languages, including Hebrew, and then tried to market it in Arab countries.

Religious and cultural differences are constantly getting global companies into trouble. Even when a firm is well intentioned, its actions can backfire. McDonald's Corporation is a case in point. When the World Cup was being hosted in Britain, McDonald's decided to put the national flags of all 24 competitors on its hamburger bags. The bags looked good and provided an international image appreciated by most people, but were considered offensive by many Muslims. It turned out that Saudi Arabia's team was in the competition and on their national flag is the Arabic passage, "There is no God but Allah, and Mohammed is his Prophet." Islamic leaders complained that these words should not be crumpled up and thrown into the trash. McDonald's ended up replacing 2 million bags. A well-known North American brewer encountered similar problems when it put those same flags on its bottles to highlight the same World Cup tournament. Not only was the Arabic passage visible, it was on a product Islamic people should avoid—beer. The bottles had to be recalled.

Although many people do not realize it, the swastika symbol was not created by the Nazis. In fact, it has been used for centuries as a symbol of good luck in many countries. In India, M.P. Been Products has been using the symbol on many of its packages as a sort of company logo. However, when its managers decided to launch a new beer described as "German Pilsner," the combination of the beer name and the swastika on the same label was not well received.

Another example of offensive packaging is when a well-known rock band produced an album cover that portrayed two naked children sitting on a teeter-totter. This album cover was found to be so highly offensive to the Japanese community that it was banned from Japan.

U.S.-made medical containers drew a great deal of unwanted attention when they were used in Great Britain. The containers carried the instructions: "Take off top and push in bottom." This message, considered harmless in the United States, bore very sexual and humorous connotations to the British. Needless to say, the containers were soon modified.

In areas where many of the people are illiterate, the label usually displays a picture of what the package contains. This very logical practice proved to be quite perplexing to one big company. It tried to sell baby food in an African nation by using its regular label that showed a baby and stated the type of baby food in the jar. Unfortunately, the local population took one look at the labels and interpreted them to mean the jars contained ground-up babies! Sales, of course, were terrible.

Some European dry soup producers have solved their marketing problems in the United States by altering their labels. Rather than trying to change the product, they merely developed different uses for the product and stated this on the package label. U.S. and European dried soups are packaged identically but labeled differently. The U.S. package emphasizes the use of the product as a sauce or dip. As expected, U.S. sales were much better once the firms stressed the non-soup use.

Even something as innocuous as a wrapping can cause trouble. A New York exporter agreed to send some products to an Arab country and thoughtlessly wrapped the goods in local newspapers for shipment. The customer was arrested and his goods confiscated when the Arab customs inspectors opened up the packages and found that the wrappings used were Jewish newspapers.

Another U.S. firm also blundered in the Middle East. A carefully detailed business proposal that had required a great deal of preparation effort was sent to Saudi Arabia. The proposal, an excellent one, was bound with a pigskin cover and so was never even read! (Muslims are required to avoid pig products.)

The use of numbers provides another source of blunders. Each country has its own special lucky and unlucky numbers and using the wrong number can indeed be unlucky. A U.S. golf ball manufacturer, for example, tried to sell golf balls, packaged in groups of four, to the Japanese. Problems arose because the pronunciation of the word "four" in Japanese also sounds like the Japanese word for "death". The number four, therefore, is considered undesirable, and items grouped into fours simply don't sell well. (The number seven is a particularly tricky number. It is considered good luck in many countries, but bad luck in others. It even has magical connotations in parts of Africa.)

U.S. airlines with routes between Japan and Hawaii initially experienced very erratic success. Some days the flights were fully booked while other days the planes flew nearly empty. It took some time, but the airlines eventually figured out the problem. Apparently, the Japanese have traditional days that are considered good for weddings. These "lucky days" are naturally followed by honeymoons, and Hawaii is a favored destination. In order to even out the flying load, the airlines began offering discounts for the days when the honeymooners were not flying.

Color

The choice of package and product coloring can be tricky. Sometimes companies have failed to sell their products overseas and have never known why. Often the reason was a simple one: the product or its container was merely an inappropriate color.

Green, for instance, is often associated with disease in countries that have dense, green jungles but is associated with cosmetics by the French, Dutch, and Swedes. Various colors represent death. Black signifies death to Americans and many Europeans, while in Japan and many other Asian countries, white represents death. Latin Americans generally associate purple with death, but dark red is the appropriate mourning color along the Ivory Coast. And even though white is the color representing death to some; it expresses joy to those living in Ghana. In many countries, bright colors such as yellow and orange express joy. To most of the world, blue is thought to be a masculine color, but it is not as manly as red in the United Kingdom or France and in Iran blue represents an undesirable color. Although pink is believed to be the foremost feminine color by Americans, most of the rest of the world considers yellow to be the most feminine color. Red is felt to be blasphemous in some African countries but is generally considered to be a color reflecting wealth or luxury elsewhere. A red circle has been successfully used on many packages sold in Latin America, but it is unpopular in some parts of Asia, where it conjures up images of the Japanese flag.

Pictures of flowers can be found on many package labels, but there, too, caution is required. Certain flowers and their colors can convey hidden messages. In France and many countries that have experienced a British influence, the white lily is often used for funerals. Mexicans, though, use lilies to lift superstitious spells. A purple flower symbolizes death to a Brazilian while yellow flowers represent death or disrespect in Mexico. In France and the Soviet Union, however, the yellow flower signifies infidelity.

United Airlines had start-up problems with its initial flights from Hong Kong. It seems that the company handed out white carnations without realizing that, to many Asians, such flowers represent death and bad luck. Thus, they soon switched to red carnations.

SUMMARY

Product and package modifications are often required to enhance a product's appeal to the foreign consumer. Sometimes the alterations are minor; other times they are more complex. Market testing can help a firm avoid the entry of an inappropriate product; the failure to initiate such studies or develop thorough ones has led a number of companies to blunder.

In all fairness to multinational firms, however, market tests can be quite tricky to initiate and conduct. It is difficult indeed to "cover all the bases," and one of the hardest tasks is the identification of the proper testing locations. Since firms cannot always afford to test each product everywhere: sample areas are normally identified as being representative of a country or region. Some companies have used an area of France for their west European test market; others have used Belgium. Each firm must determine the region most appropriate for its product. This is no easy task. In fact, a combination of locations may be necessary. Wherever these places are, though, they must be found, because market testing is essential.

CHAPTER 3

Names

- Product Names
- Company Names
- Summary

Names

Shakespeare once queried, "What's in a name?" A number of business people, after a bit of international marketing, might appropriately respond, "More than you might think." Many companies have discovered that even something as seemingly innocuous as a name can prove to be insulting and embarrassing. Both product and company names can fall prey to such troubles.

Product Names

Product names often take on various unintended and hidden meanings. The experience of a major soap maker serves as a classic example. When this company was considering a name for a new soap powder it wished to market internationally, it wisely ran a translation test of the proposed name in 50 major languages. In English and most of the major European languages, the name meant "dainty." In other tongues, however, it did not translate so appropriately. In Gaelic, it became "song," in Flemish it meant "aloof," and it said "horse" in the language of one African tribe. In Persia, the name was translated as "hazy" or "dim-witted," and to the Koreans the name sounded like a person out of his mind. Finally, in all of the Slavic languages the name was considered obscene and offensive. Naturally, the proposed name was hastily abandoned. This experience, though, demonstrates the importance of a name and how carefully it should be considered prior to the introduction of a product.

Unusual problems

"Golden Harp Superior Pilsner" is hard enough to say in English, but it is even more difficult to say if English is not your mother tongue. In Malaysia (where they do not even have harps), the words are very difficult to pronounce and certainly do not sound like the name of a beer. Therefore, Ogilvy & Mather shortened the product's name to "Goldie" and used a sexy blonde to promote the brew. The problem was that the label still read "Golden Harp Superior Pilsner" so, when Malaysians ordered a Goldie, all they usually got from the bartender was a blank stare. The product was eventually withdrawn.

Today, more and more firms are seeking assistance in the hope of avoiding costly and embarrassing mistakes. Even the largest and most sophisticated firms are not immune to the difficulties of product-name interpretation. For example, when the Coca-Cola Company was planning its strategy for marketing in China in the 1920s, it wanted to introduce its product with the English pronunciation of "Coca-Cola." A translator developed a group of Chinese characters which, when pronounced, sounded like the product name. These characters were placed on the cola bottles and marketed. Was it any wonder that sales levels were low? The characters actually translated to "a wax-flattened mare" or "bite the wax tadpole." Since the product was new, sound was unimportant to the consumers; meaning was vital. Today Coca-Cola is again marketing its cola in China. The new characters used on the bottle translate to "happiness in the mouth." From its first marketing attempts Coca-Cola learned a valuable lesson in international marketing.

Olympia reportedly tried to introduce a photocopier in Chile under the name "Roto". The copiers, however, did not sell well. Why? Two possible explanations: (1) *roto* is the Spanish word for "broken", and (2) *roto* is the word used to delineate the lowest class in Chile.

One of Japan's largest tourist agencies suffered the perils of a misinterpreted name problem. The confusion occurred when it first entered the English-speaking markets and began receiving requests for unusual sex tours. It finally discovered the reason was its name, Kinki Nippon Tourist Company. The owners changed the name.

Some car manufacturers have experienced comparable situations. In fact, problems often develop with the names used in international automobile promotions. For example, difficulties arose during the translation of the name of the U.S. car "Randan." Apparently this name was interpreted by some Japanese to mean "idiot." The American Motors Corporation's "Matador" usually conjures up images of virility and strength, but in Puerto Rico it means "killer"—not a favorable connotation in a place with high traffic fatality rates.

Toyota has been a very successful international company, but it too has had some problems. Its rather popular MR2, for example, has sold well in several countries, but has had troubles in France because the name MR2 is often pronounced as *merde*, meaning human waste.

"Apache" pickup trucks do not sell well to most American Indians—that is, except to Apaches. This type of problem is not unique to Chevy, nor is it new. Studebaker introduced the "Dictator" back in 1927 but had to discontinue the line in 1936 when politics in Italy and Germany drew world attention.

Initial sales of Nissan's sports car, the "Fair Lady", were so disappointing in the United States that management decided to investigate the cause. The conclusion: the name Fair Lady was not sporty enough. Thus, the name was changed to "240 Z" and the car became one of the most successful Nissan has ever launched.

In 2003, General Motors decided to rename its Buick "LaCrosse" in Canada. Why? Well, in Quebec, *la crosse* is slang for masturbation.

Ford encountered problems with some of its cars as well. It introduced a low-cost truck, the "Fiera," into some of the less developed countries. Unfortunately the name meant "ugly old woman" in Spanish. Needless to say, this name did not encourage sales. Ford also experienced slow sales when it introduced a top-of-the-line automobile, the "Comet," in Mexico under the name "Caliente." The puzzlingly low sales levels were finally understood when Ford discovered that *caliente* is slang for a streetwalker. Additional headaches were reportedly experienced when Ford's "Pinto" was briefly introduced in Brazil under its English name. The name was speedily changed to "Corcel" (which means "horse" in Portuguese) after Ford discovered that the Portuguese slang translation of *pinto* is a "small male appendage."

The naming of a new automobile model to be marketed in Germany by Rolls-Royce was a difficult undertaking. The company felt that the English name "Silver Mist" was very appealing but discovered that the name would undoubtedly not capture the German market as hoped. In German, the translated meaning of "mist" is actually "excrement," and the Germans could not possibly have found such a name attractive. Unfortunately, the Sunbeam Corporation did not learn of this particular translation problem in time and attempted to enter the German market advertising its new mist-producing hair curling iron, the "Mist-Stick." As should have been expected, the Germans had no interest in a "dung" or "manure" wand.

When Sharwood's launched its latest product range in the United Kingdom, it promised that the "deliciously rich" sauces based on a traditional northern Indian method of cooking would "change the way consumers make curry." Sharwood's was so confident that its new "Bundh" sauces would be a hit that it backed the launch with a huge $14.2 million television advertising campaign. Unfortunately, *bundh* in Punjabi has an altogether less savoury meaning—the nearest English translation is "ass".

Jolly Green Giant products were incorrectly translated into Arabic to say that they were products from the "intimidating Green Ogre".

Bacardi developed and launched a fruity drink and named it "Pavian," thinking this sounded exotic and desirable. It wasn't popular in Germany, though, because *Pavian* means "baboon" there.

In the early 1980s, a German beer company launched a new brand in West Africa and named it "Eku." Sales were uneven, and it took the firm two years to figure out the cause. Foreigners and some local tribe members purchased the beer, but one important tribe totally avoided it. Apparently *eku* was the local slang word in that tribe for excrement. As word spread, members of other tribes and even the foreigners started drinking it less. In the meantime, however, more than a few natives enjoyed watching outsiders consume Eku. Naturally, the name was eventually dropped.

Firms occasionally try to enter the foreign market promoting a product bearing an untranslated name. Sometimes this tactic works, but other times it does not work as well as expected. At least one global firm can attest to this. The company consistently marketed one of its pieces of equipment under the name "Grab Bucket." To its chagrin, the firm learned that in Germany it was actually advertising the sale of cemetery plot flowers. In German, the word *Grab* is interpreted as *grave*, and *bucket* is pronounced like *bouquet*. So, because of these linguistic anomalies, the company did not appear to be selling what it thought at all.

When Vicks cough drops were first introduced to the German market, the company was upset to learn that the German pronunciation of "v" is "f," which results in the guttural equivalent of "sexual penetration." "Puff" tissues did not do well in Germany, either. *Puff*, in German, is a colloquial term for a house of prostitution. (In fact, most British weren't impressed with the name, either, since "puff" is a very derogatory term in England for a homosexual.) Ford Motor Company introduced the "Probe" in Germany, where Probe translates as a "test" or "rehearsal," which caused customers to think they were buying a test car, instead of the real thing. The most ironic part of this example is that Ford has a fully staffed German subsidiary, again emphasizing the need for checking and double-checking names as thoroughly as possible before introduction, to avoid blunders.

Many other companies have suffered similar pitfalls. A U.S. company was taken by surprise when it introduced its product in Latin America and learned that the name of the product meant "jackass oil" in Spanish. Another well-intentioned firm sold shampoo in Brazil under the name "Evitol." Little did it realize that it was claiming to be selling a "dandruff contraceptive." A manufacturing company sold its machines in the Soviet Union under the name "Bardak"—a word that signifies a brothel in Russian. One U.S. product failed to capture the Swedish market when the product name was translated to "enema," which the product was not. Kellogg has done fairly well with its sales of cereals overseas, but even it had to rename its "Bran Buds" cereal in Sweden when the company discovered that the name translates roughly as "burned farmer." Parker Pen sells a pen in most countries under the name "Jotter." However, it wisely uses other names in some Latin American markets, because "Jotter" sometimes means a jockstrap.

A Finnish brewery introduced two new beverages in the United States—"Koff" beer and "Siff" beer. Is it any wonder that sales were sluggish? Another name, unappealing to Americans, can be found on the package of a delicious chocolate and fruit product sold in the European deli. The chocolate concoction has the undesirable English name "Zit!" "Sic" (a French soft drink), "Super Piss" (a Finnish product for unfreezing car doors), and "Bum" (a Spanish potato chip) will probably not be sold in the United States either.

Other product names that would prove to be a problem in the United States are "Polio," a Czech laundry detergent; "Cat Wetty," a Japanese moistened hand towel; "Homo," an Asian fish sausage; "Swine," Chinese chocolates; "Ass Glue," a Chinese glue; "Last Climax," Japanese paper tissues; and "Creap Creamy Powder," a Japanese coffee creamer.

The Chinese attempted to introduce products to the U.S. market using brand names such as "White Elephant" brand batteries; "Sea Cucumber" brand shirts; "Maxipuke" playing cards (which in Chinese, *pu ke*, is pronounced in two syllables and means poker); as well as "Pansy" brand men's underwear.

A Japanese company tried to sell its baby powder in the United States under the name "Skinababe." Not surprisingly, sales were very low.

An Australian brewer sells a popular beer in Australia by the name of "XXXX" which is pronounced "Four X." The company planned to export this beer to the United States until it learned that the Americans were already familiar with "Fourex"—a brand of condoms.

The reported troubles of a U.S. company that markets "Pet" milk serves as another example. This firm reportedly experienced difficulties introducing its product in French-speaking areas. It seems that the word *pet* in French means, among other things, "to break wind." And had Colgate-Palmolive attempted to gain market entry with its "Cue" toothpaste in French-speaking regions, it too would have encountered comparable problems. *Cue* is a pornographic word in French.

An American woman will long remember her international experience with Coca-Cola. She was dispensing sample tasters of "Fresca" soda pop when she unintentionally elicited a great deal of laughter from passersby. She only later realized the cause when she discovered that in Mexican slang the word *fresca* means "lesbian."

Close examination of foreign markets and language differences are necessary and should be required before a product's domestically successful name is introduced abroad. Unfortunately, this simple warning is sometimes neglected in a company's enthusiasm to plunge into overseas marketing operations.

Manufacturers often assume that products that have enjoyed domestic success will naturally receive the same reception overseas. However, this is not always the case, as the following examples demonstrate. Princess Housewares, a large U.S. appliance manufacturer, introduced a line of electric housewares in the German market. The company's brand name, well known and highly regarded in the United States, was relatively unknown in Germany. Its name, though, which had a definite American sound, turned out to be a real drawback to sales, as the German consumers disliked the American association.

Name adaptations sometimes prove to be winners; other times they do not. The Johnson Wax Company successfully introduced its product "Pledge" in Germany under the name of "Pronto," but problems arose when the product entered the market in the Netherlands as "Pliz." In Dutch, the pronunciation of Pliz sounds like "piss." Understandably, it was rather difficult for the customer of the conventional Dutch grocery store to ask for the product.

Sometimes the required change in the product name is a rather simple one. Wrigley, for example, merely altered the spelling of its "Spearmint" chewing gum to "Speermint" to aid in the German pronunciation of the flavor. "Maxwell House" proved slightly more difficult. The name was changed to "Maxwell Kaffee" in Germany, "Legal" in France, and "Monky" in Spain.

As evidenced, firms have blundered by changing product names and by failing to alter names. This is not to say, however, that one is "damned if you do and damned if you do not." Adequate name assessments prior to market introduction can reduce potential name blunders.

Obscene meanings

Inappropriate product names sometimes prove to be quite humorous, but in a number of cases, the names have actually borne fairly obscene implications and connotations. A few illustrations of this type of blunder are cited below.

Bird's Eye considered itself quite fortunate when it discovered that a proposed name for one of its fish food products was inappropriate. Wisely, the company decided against the name when it uncovered that the name translated to "genitals." Not all firms have been so lucky, however. A well-known oil company was caught in an embarrassing situation when it learned of the "indecent" name it had chosen for its products. The company established operations in Indonesia and manufactured machinery displaying the name "Nonox." One can imagine the firm's discomfort when it was informed that Nonox sounded similar to the Javanese slang word *nonok*—a word comparable to the U.S. idiom for female "private parts."

Obviously the employees who proposed the name "Joni" for a new facial cream which was to be marketed in India had never read the erotic Indian classic *Kama Sutra*. If they had, they would surely have known that the Hindu word *joni* represents the most intimate areas of the female body.

The example of a vitamin product introduced in South America serves as a final illustration of how product names can unintentionally become obscenities. In this case, a company introduced its vitamins as "Fundavit" and boasted that they satisfied the fundamental vitamin requirements. The name had to be modified when the firm learned that *fundola* in Spanish stands for the rear end of an attractive young female.

Other offensive names

As illustrated, certain product name choices can create embarrassing situations for companies when the names are interpreted as indecencies. On occasion, a company chooses a name which, although not obscene, turns out to be in poor taste and offensive to certain groups of people. One example is the name "Black Nikka" chosen for a brand of Japanese whisky sold in the United States and found to be demeaning by some black Americans. Consider also the bold experiment in international marketing that brought together the state-controlled tobacco monopolies of five countries (France, Italy, Portugal, Austria, and Japan) to launch a major promotion of a new brand of cigarettes, "Champagne." This venture proved to be an embarrassment to the French government, and the case wound up in the international law courts with the French champagne producers in a fury. These producers claimed that the use of "Champagne" as a brand name "is deplorable, and the connection with health hazards may permanently damage our image."[1]

Reebok unveiled a new women's sneaker named "Incubus." In medieval folklore Incubus was a demon who ravished women in their sleep. Reebok was forced to discontinue the shoe.

Company Names

Product names are not the only ones that can generate company blunders. If a firm name is misinterpreted or incorrectly translated, it too can cause humorous, obscene, offensive, or unexpected situations. A number of examples are described in the following paragraphs.

Colonel Sanders (KFC) experienced resistance marketing its chicken in Germany because some folks connected the word "Colonel" with the U.S. military that is not popular with all Germans. And because Brazilians have trouble pronouncing "Kentucky Fried Chicken," the name "Sanders" was used there.

A private Egyptian airline, Misair, proved to be rather unpopular with the French nationals. Could the fact that the name, which when pronounced meant "misery" in French, have contributed to the airline's plight? Another airline trying to gain acceptance in Australia only complicated matters when it chose the firm name "Emu." The emu is an Australian bird that is incapable of flying. But Emu was not the only company to run into snags while conducting business in Australia. The AMF Corporation was forced to change its name. Why? Because AMF is the official designation for the Australian military forces. Similarly, Sears (originally Sears Roebuck & Co.) was forbidden to use its name in Spain. The company commanded respect and enjoyed a good reputation there, but since the Castillian Spanish pronunciation of Sears sounded much like "Seat" (the name of Spain's largest car manufacturer), Seat forced Sears to incorporate the name Roebuck on all its products.

As a final illustration, consider the trade magazine that promoted giftware and launched a worldwide circulation effort. The magazine used the word *gift* in its title and as part of its name. When it was later revealed that *Gift* is the German word for "poison," a red-faced publishing executive supposedly retorted that the Germans should simply find a new word for poison!

Of course, not all companies have been forced to change their names. In fact, some of them have traveled quite well. Kodak may be the most famous example. A research team deliberately "developed" this name after carefully searching for a word which was pronounceable everywhere but had no specific meaning anywhere. Exxon is another such name that was reportedly accepted only after a lengthy and expensive computer-assisted search.

SUMMARY

Multinational corporations have experienced many unexpected troubles concerning company or product names, and even attempts to alter names have led to blunders. It should be evident that careful planning and study of the potential market are necessary, as name adaptation can be every bit as important as product or package modification.

CHAPTER 4

Marketing

- Promotions
- Pricing
- Summary

CHAPTER 4

Marketing

The field of marketing has probably experienced the most corporate headaches. The old adage, "if something can go wrong, it will," seems especially true for marketing managers; they have undoubtedly blundered every single marketing task imaginable.

Early blunders often occurred because people forgot that cultures vary from country to country. Unfortunately, this error continues to be made. A print advertisement for men's cologne, for example, pictured a man and his dog in an American rural setting. The picture was well accepted in America but was not effective when used in northern Africa. The advertiser simply assumed that the American "man's best friend" was loved everywhere when, in fact, Muslims usually consider dogs to be either signs of bad luck or symbols of uncleanliness. Neither interpretation helped sales of the cologne.

Procter & Gamble blundered in Japan when trying to sell "Camay" soap. It seems that it aired a popular European television advertisement showing a woman bathing. In the ad, her husband enters the bathroom and touches her approvingly. The Japanese, however, considered this behavior to be inappropriate and in poor taste for television. Such ads are no longer used in Japan and P&G is now doing much better there.

A well-known American designer tried to launch a new fragrance in Latin America. The advertising message emphasized the perfume's fresh camellia scent. Naturally, sales were slow there because camellias are flowers used for funerals in most of Latin America.

Procter & Gamble's original Japanese promotion of "Cheer" laundry detergent boasted that the detergent was effective at "all water temperatures." The slogan proved successful in the United States because Americans wash their laundry in many different temperatures depending on the preference of the consumer. However, the Japanese wash most clothes in cold water, so the promotion was almost meaningless to them. Procter & Gamble changed its approach and ran ads touting Cheer's superior cleaning in cold water. Now Cheer sells much better in Japan.

Not all blunders, of course, are due to the erroneous assumption that what works at home will always work abroad also. Sometimes, the promotional campaign is just launched at the wrong time.

Timing is one of the most critical elements in the launching of a new product. Most firms understand this and also recognize that various cultures perceive time differently. Since some nationalities are more conscious of time factors than others, extra time must often be allocated and care given to assure that everything is completed as scheduled. One firm aware of these constraints properly timed everything, or so it thought. Various types of promotional activities were arranged for its product's market entries, but one thing was overlooked— the product. Because someone forgot to assure its availability, all of the expensive, well-planned promotions became meaningless.

The Israel Government Tourist Office wisely suspended an ad campaign in the Netherlands that proclaimed that Tel Aviv and Jerusalem were only "a stone's throw" apart. The timing of the ad was unfortunate, as real stone throwing was actually occurring in the country at the time.

Promotions

Promotional efforts often misfire; some downfalls, though, are more predictable than others. A cosmetics firm attempted to sell its lipstick in Japan using a television ad that depicted Nero coming to life just as a pretty woman wearing the lipstick strolled by. This was a hard sell because the Japanese women did not know of Nero. If a firm decides to use historical figures in promotional campaigns, it is well advised to first consider using locally known historical figures.

Hoover vacuum cleaners could not "sweep up the mess" from a recent sales promotion blunder considered one of the biggest in corporate history. The costly and embarrassing blunder was an offer by Hoover Europe for two free overseas airline tickets to anybody in Britain or Ireland who bought one of its vacuum cleaners. The problem was that the tickets were worth more than the cost of the cleaner. This promotion turned into a court battle when disgruntled customers never received their flights. Hoover tried to attach conditions to the deal, in an effort to recover from the error. After spending $72 million on flying 220,000 people they hoped to end the case. But over 365,000 other customers still had not flown. As a result three top European executives were fired.

In a different type of case, a company formed a joint venture with an Asian firm. Both companies believed everything to be in order. Their plan included a large production run and a simultaneous, large promotional effort. The production process ran smoothly, but the expected promotional efforts never materialized. Each company had assumed that the other would coordinate and pay for all promotional activities. In fact, each firm simply assumed the customs of its own country's business practices and was not prepared to accept the other country's norm. Neither company would have agreed to the venture had it thought that it would be responsible for promotion costs. The promotion was never undertaken, and the joint venture eventually broke up.

Potential problems of ill-thought campaigns by global brand managers and advertisers who advertise in the United States can still have potential negative global ramifications. The U.S. cosmetics firm Clinique had to stop running a print ad for its "Elixir" perfume when Thailand's government sent a letter of protest to the company complaining the ad was an insult to Buddhists. The perfume ad, which ran in *Vogue* and other U.S. fashion magazines, depicts a snake crawling over the head of an image of the lord Buddha. Clinique reportedly pulled the ad and sent a letter of apology to the Thai ambassador in Washington, expressed its shock to hear about any possible negative perceptions presented by the picture.

One of United's promotional campaigns used the slogan, "We know the Orient." In the ads, the names of Far Eastern countries were printed below the pictures of foreign coins. Sadly, the slogan was not very convincing—the coins and countries did not match up.

A company must be especially careful when entering a new market with a new product or service. The old saying, "you only get a chance to make a first impression once," has never been truer. A blunder at the start is hard to recover from. America-on-line (AOL) learned this lesson. In fact, AOL reportedly had several problems while launching a new promotional campaign in Brazil. Hundreds of would-be new users were mistakenly given music CDs rather than the intended CD-ROMs needed to start up AOL's service. However, as unlikely as this may seem, they may have been the lucky ones. It turned out that those new subscribers receiving the "correct" CD-ROMs discovered that some of their computer programs were changed without warning. Web browsers were altered and home pages were replaced. AOL certainly did not make a good first impression with these people.

Another U.S. corporation believed it had developed a good promotional plan when it decided to distribute simulated old coins displaying the company logo. To make the coins appear a bit more realistic, the company placed a monetary value on them and, to avoid any chance of claims of counterfeiting, it used the obviously phony value of $1 billion. The coins were passed out at a trade show in West Germany but, to the company's surprise, the coins seemed to anger the locals. Apparently the Germans felt that the company was trying to show off American wealth, and they resented this impression. The coins would have been more effective if they had displayed some denomination of the German mark.

As the women's movement continues to gain momentum, more and more firms are realizing they must scrutinize all promotional efforts carefully to make sure that their advertisements are not offensive to women. Failure to recognize potential problems can cause later difficulties (such as product boycotts). Quebec, for example, now has a review board that monitors possibly offensive advertisements. In 1981, it presented its first "awards" for sexism. One "award" was conferred for a Sony and La Place stereo shop ad. This ad portrayed a big-busted woman, her nipples showing through her T-shirt, roller-skating while holding her Sony tape deck. The review jury found the promotion offensive, as there was no connection between the woman and the product being advertised. Another "award" went to Procter & Gamble for its 30-second "Mr. Clean" television commercial. In this ad, a little girl is shown cleaning up her brother's mess as he watches. The jury felt the company was reinforcing the old sex role stereotypes that housecleaning is women's work and the women should serve the men.

An advertising campaign for Fiat's "Cinquecento" automobile backfired in Spain when they sent anonymous love letters to women in an attempt to attract the "independent, modern, working woman." Instead, *El Mundo* newspaper reported that the letters made women feel threatened, as if they were being stalked by a psychopath, and created jealous scenes between spouses. The letters were printed on pink paper, personally addressed, complimented and invited the recipient to indulge in "a little adventure" after noticing "how [you] glanced interestedly in my direction."

BMW reportedly experienced some awkward moments a few years ago while launching its new 3-series models in Great Britain. It wanted to remind the television viewers of its proud heritage. It wanted to say that the new models are based on BMW's great tradition and experience with its previous models. BMW tried to do this by depicting the sporty car with DNA-type strings attached, but it used DNA symbols without bothering to find out much about them. For most viewers this advertisement was fine, until someone pointed out that the DNA depicted actually belonged to a slow-moving 10,000-year-old woolly mammoth (now extinct, of course). Not exactly the image desired.

Nike experienced some awkward moments in the United States when one of its television advertisements included people from various countries reportedly stating Nike's slogan—"Just do it"—in their native languages.

However, one man, a Samburu tribesman, was really saying, "I don't want these, give me big shoes." Naturally, Nike's competition made sure people learned of the error. Nike admitted that their people did not really know what the natives were saying, but one suspects that Nike will be more careful in the future.

Most people wealthy enough to afford to stay at New York's Helmsley Palace Hotel know enough about the world to know that the Taj Mahal is a mausoleum. However, that did not stop Leona Helmsley from approving a promotion that compared her hotel with the Taj Mahal. The headline stated, "In India it's the Taj Mahal. In New York it's the Helmsley Palace." It went on to proclaim, "Service and appointments fit for royalty—you—our guests."

In Chapter 2, the problem of using inappropriate product and package colors was discussed. Colors can create promotional difficulties as well. The Singer Company, for example, found it necessary to halt an elaborate outdoor ad campaign when, just prior to the campaign's introduction, the company discovered that the background color, blue, was the local color representing death. Singer was fortunate that the error was discovered when it was. Because Singer had hired local people to implement its promotional plan, the potential blunder was averted.

The McDonnell Douglas Corporation experienced unexpected difficulties with a brochure that it planned to distribute to potential aircraft customers in India. The promotional material depicted turbaned men, but the photos were not well received. The company had used old *National Geographic* pictures and had overlooked the fact that Pakistani men, not Indians, were wearing the turbans!

The "Marlboro" man projects a strong masculine image in the United States and in Europe. Attempts to use it were unsuccessful in Hong Kong, where the totally urban people did not identify at all with horseback riding in the countryside. So Philip Morris quickly changed its ad to reflect a Hong Kong-style Marlboro man. He is still a virile cowboy, but he is younger, better dressed, and owns a truck and the land he's standing on.

Conducting business in a communist country is especially tricky. A slip of the tongue or pen can prove fatal. Even the name of the country can cause trouble, since the names given to some countries by the West are usually different than those used by the countries themselves. The failure to use the proper country name is often considered an insensitive or offensive act. For instance, the English-language catalog of a Swedish firm had to be changed because the catalog cited "North Korea" instead of the "People's Republic of Korea."

A geographical blunder occurred when France introduced a new postage stamp in 1991, bearing a picture of Easter Island and claiming it to be a French territory; the Chilean government protested, since it is part of Chile. Blunders like this really weaken relations between countries, especially with Latin America, where relationships are of vital importance.

United Airlines finally received permission in 1982 to initiate flights to Japan only to have its introductory campaign crash. United's public relations people in the United States tried to show customers the company's new route. Unfortunately, the map they used failed to include a major Japanese island. The Japanese are extremely sensitive about their territorial claims (and losses), and were highly offended by such a map. To them it showed ignorance or, perhaps worse, insensitivity. Although only a few copies of the map ever existed, the blunder made headline news in the second largest Japanese newspaper, and drew a hasty apology from

United. As United admitted, the mistake would never have happened if its staff in Tokyo had a chance to look at the map before its release.

Americans are not the only managers who face the challenges of marketing internationally. In one edition of *Newsweek* an image ad from STET, the Italian telephone company, was shown promoting itself as global. It showed a picture of a Chinese temple on a lakeshore, with a reflection in the water of a Roman arch. The effect was somewhat lost, however, because the image of the temple was flipped from left to right, and therefore all the Chinese writing on the temple was in mirror-image characters. This did not impress those who could read Chinese.

Several firms have tried to use old, reliable promotional methods in countries where they simply do not work. Billboard advertisements are perfectly legal in most parts of the Middle East, for example, but this does not mean they should be used. Many companies have tried to employ billboards, but instead of advertising their product, they have merely exposed their lack of awareness of local weather conditions. In the Middle East environment, billboards often last less than two weeks.

Companies have even been known to promote their products using the wrong language. In Dubai, for example, only 10 percent of the population speak Arabic. The remaining 90 percent of the people originate from Pakistan, India, Iran, or elsewhere. Several European and U.S. firms, however, have assumed that all Middle Eastern countries are primarily populated with Arabic-speaking people and so have promoted their products only in Arabic.

Time magazine ran a Spanish-language ad in its Brazilian edition. Someone must have forgotten that they speak Portuguese in Brazil, not Spanish!

Misunderstandings

In many cases, the language of the promotional effort is correct but the message is simply not effective. It is one thing to use the right language, but it is quite another to use it so that the intended message is properly communicated. As a classic illustration, consider the company that rented space on a wall beside the main road leading from the airport into Buenos Aires. The following message was placed on the wall; "With [brand name] you'd be there already." Just one slight problem existed: The message was misunderstood because it was placed on the wall of a cemetery.

Isuzu reflected a cultural gap of knowledge when it used a line in a television advertisement for its "Trooper" utility vehicle that said, "You don't have to buy the farm to get one." This phrase was, unfortunately, an old aviation expression implying that owners of the trucks might "crash and burn."

It may be easy to place a message in a slightly wrong location, but Amalie Refining was off by quite a few miles. One of its Spanish-language billboards somehow landed along the roadside in Knoxville, Tennessee.

Arabic writing is very sacred to the Islamic community. Several blunders are prime examples. One such example was Arabic writing printed on bathroom products. Croscill Home Fashions, in New York, had no idea that the pattern contained words at all. The company spent between $10,000 to $20,000 to change the design when it found out from the Council on American–Islamic Relations that it was considered undignified. Specific bath items were printed with writing recognizable as a common Islamic phrase, "There is no victor but God." It was considered in poor taste on bath towels and wash cloths because they are items used to wipe the body.

The fashion industry learned a lesson in an unfortunate error that was not intended as an insult when Lagerfeld introduced a new fashion collection in 1994 that borrowed Arabic script to decorate some low-cut evening gowns. When the Muslim leaders saw a photo of one of the Chanel dance dresses they commented that the patterns on the dresses were incidental examples of a "new Occidental crusade against Muslims in order to annihilate them." Lagerfeld was forced to remove the dresses from the Chanel collection.

Nike attempted to use Arabic script on athletic shoes. The script resembled the word "Allah," the word for God. Muslims hold holy symbols as sacred and not to be represented on shoes that will be covered in dirt, walked on and then disposed of. The logo was meant to look like flames displayed on the shoes and sold during the summer, with names like "Air Bakin'," "Air Melt," "Air Grill," and "Air B-Que." The blunder was discovered by the Council on American–Islamic Relations who demanded that Nike apologize for the use of the logo. The company admitted to recognizing the error prior to the release of the shoes and regretted any misunderstanding. In addition, a member of the Muslim organization wanted Nike to also participate in sensitivity-training programs about Islamic culture.

A firm at an international trade fair committed a different type of location error. In order to keep people out of a restricted area of its booth, the company displayed a sign depicting an open, flat hand with all fingers pointing up on a swinging door. To the company's surprise, the idea backfired. The local people interpreted the symbol to mean they should place their hands there and push the door open.

Symbols or logos have caused troubles for other companies as well. A U.S. firm marketing in Brazil found itself a bit embarrassed when it used a large deer as a sign for masculinity. The word *deer* is a Brazilian street name for a homosexual. Another company blundered in India when it used an owl in its promotional efforts. To an Indian, the owl is a symbol for bad luck, and indeed it proved to be just that for the firm.

Muslims in Dhaka, Bangladesh went on a rampage, ransacking shoe stores because they mistook the Thom McAn logo on some sandals for the Arabic characters for "Allah." They thought the Western company was denigrating their religion. Police were called in to stop the rioting, but at least one person was killed and 50 people were wounded before it was over.

Several companies have gotten into trouble by using the traditional U.S. sign showing a hand giving the "OK" signal. It communicates the message well in the United States, but is a very vulgar sign in many countries. It's best to simply avoid using it overseas in any promotional activities or other forms of communication.

A few years ago a Japanese steel firm, Sumitomo, introduced its specialty steel pipe into the U.S. market. Sumitomo used a Tokyo-based, Japanese agency to help develop its advertisements. The steel was named "Sumitomo High Toughness," and the name was promoted by the acronym SHT in bold letters. So bold, in fact, that the full-page ads run in trade journal were three-fourths filled with SHT. Located at the bottom of the page was a short message that ended with the claim that the product "was made to match its name." The importance of local input simply cannot be overemphasized!

One laundry detergent company certainly wishes now that it had contacted a few locals before it initiated its promotional campaign in the Middle East. All of the company's advertisements pictured soiled clothes on the left, its box of soap in the middle, and clean clothes on the right. But because in that area of the world people tend to read from the right to the left, many potential customers interpreted the message to indicate the soap actually soiled the clothes.

In Seoul, senior executives at Samsung Group reportedly did not notice that a wall calendar's model for July, holding Samsung products, was wearing a see-through blouse. The wall calendar, portraying international models, was sent overseas to customers and partners as a gift. The group was informed that the calendar photo offended some Americans. The group's manager of the personnel department responded by admitting that they were unaware of the potential problem.

Even if the correct shots and words are used, problems can crop up because of incorrect intonation. Missionaries in Africa discovered this when someone finally informed them that the messages in their songs were being misunderstood. The words were correctly translated, but the tones and pitches used were not. For example, the Igbo people of Nigeria learned to sing the second verse of "Oh, come, all ye faithful." They were thought to be singing "Very God, begotten, not created," but the actual meaning was "God's pig, which is never shared." Another hymn with words of "There is no sorrow in heaven" came out "There is no egg on the bicycle."

Care must be taken even when the consumers of a foreign market speak the same language. A British and U.S. joint venture proposal ran into serious difficulties, for example, when the U.S. firm requested that certain key points be "tabled." The British firm agreed and both parties prepared for negotiations. When the British team brought up for discussion those topics that had been "tabled," both parties became highly irritated. In the United States "to table a motion" means to delay discussion of it, but in England the same phrase often means to bring the topic to the table for discussion. The

Americans had requested the exact opposite of what they had really wanted.

Similar problems were encountered by another U.S. company attempting to conduct business in Britain. The firm had effectively used the phrase "You can use no finer napkin at your dinner table" in the United States and because of economies of scale, etc., decided to use the same commercials in England. After all, Britons do speak English. To a Briton, however, an American does not speak English, but speaks "American" and uses different phrases and word meanings. Since the British word "napkin" or "nappy" actually means "diaper," the American firm was unknowingly advertising that "You could use no finer diaper at your dinner table." The ad was entertaining, but could hardly be expected to boost sales greatly.

American troubles with the English language are not limited to England, of course. One U.S. banker in Australia discovered this when he attended an important dinner given in his honor. He was invited to speak after the meal, but he certainly started off on the wrong foot when he indicated that he was "full." The subsequent nervous laughter of the other diners suggested something was wrong, so he tried to clarify the situation by saying that he was "stuffed." One can imagine his astonishment when he learned that "full" implied being drunk and that "stuffed" suggested involvement in sexual intercourse.

Strategy

Often it is the promotional strategy that runs amuck and creates the promotional blunders. Whereas some companies have appeared culturally insensitive, others have actually blundered by going to the opposite extreme.

They have tried to fake being local or have tried to play up to local nationalist pride. Dow Breweries, for instance, introduced a new beer in Quebec, Canada, called "Kebec." The promotion incorporated the Canadian flag and attempted to evoke nationalistic pride. Dow's strategy backfired, however, when major local groups protested the "profane" use of "sacred" symbols. The campaign was halted within 15 days.

In an eager effort to get out "good news" fast, Thunderbird blundered in a press release in 1997 by saying it was the oldest management school in the world in a release handed to the Academy of International Business members in Mexico for its annual meeting. The problem was it wasn't true—as most readers knew. People were offended because of the missing word "international" as it should have said it was the oldest international management school.

Similarly, when McDonald's used an illustration of Mexico's national flag on its place mats in 1988, the company drew the ire of local authorities. The Mexicans simply did not approve of catsup being splattered all over one of its national symbols, so the place mats were confiscated. The offense, of course, was unintentional, but McDonald's apologized anyway.

Alka-Seltzer suffered a drastic downturn in its market share and profits when its new German owner, Bayer, decided to abandon Alka-Seltzer's traditional identity as a cure for blue-collar hangovers and tried to pitch the product as a remedy for young professional stress. Bayer eventually realized that it misunderstood the U.S. market so it switched back and recovered.

A French beer company experienced difficulty trying to enter the U.S. market when it projected itself as American. Its decision to portray its imported beer as locally brewed was not a wise one because the U.S. market was already flooded with local beers. The company, realizing its error, now does well promoting its beer as an import.

Products sell better when the promotions emphasize what the consumer considers important. Tires can be used as an example. Tire safety is stressed in Britain, durability and mileage are emphasized in the United States and agile performance is considered important in Germany. Goodyear learned this lesson early and has been successful selling the same tire in all three markets using different messages.

General Mills, producer of "Betty Crocker" brand cakes, tried to introduce cake mixes to the Japanese. They found out that most Japanese households did not have an oven, and preferred to buy cakes. Market research revealed that almost every household did have a rice cooker so General Mills developed a product called "Cakeron," a cake mix to be cooked in the rice cooker. Sales went well during the introduction of Cakeron. But when sales dwindled, market research revealed that since rice was often left over and saved in the rice cooker, baking cakes was inconvenient. What was important to the Japanese household was the consumption of rice. In addition, the cake mixes often left an aftertaste in the rice cooker. The comparison was drawn that a Japanese cook who makes cakes in a rice cooker is like an English housewife making coffee in her teapot. This just does not happen.

Multinationals, therefore, must consider varying pro-motional tactics. Volvo has applied this concept quite successfully. The company has emphasized economy, durability, and safety in the United States; status and leisure in France; performance in Germany; and safety in Switzerland. Price is considered to be a critical variable to Mexican consumers, but quality is of more importance to Venezuelans.

Test markets can be used to evaluate promotional campaigns, but results are not necessarily fail-safe. U.S. companies often use Puerto Rico as a typical Latin American test market. Although Puerto Rico is a convenient, almost barrier-free, Spanish-speaking market and thus an appealing test market, the people of each Latin American country have their own unique tastes and preferences. Therefore, firms must realize that the success of a promotional strategy in Puerto Rico does not necessarily assure success in all Latin American countries. All that should be gleaned with confidence from a positive result in Puerto Rico is that the strategy is worth testing in the country under consideration. Major blunders have occurred when this second testing procedure was skipped. The managers of one company, for example, were so excited by the impressive results experienced in Puerto Rico that they shipped large quantities of their product, a hair fixer, to Argentina. Sales were practically nonexistent even though the commercials so successful in Puerto Rico were used. Sales improved only after the local sales manager convinced the company to alter the ads and direct them towards a more European-type customer.

Unilever experienced a somewhat unique type of promotional problem. The company marketed a popular detergent, "Radion," in Germany. It also sold the same basic product in Austria but marketed it under a different brand name. Because Germans and Austrians both speak German and are often exposed to each other's media, consumers in each country were being introduced to what they thought were competitive products. Since the promotional campaigns developed for one country easily reached the consumers in the other country, a more efficient and effective marketing strategy would have been to use the same brand name in both countries. Had this occurred, the promotional overlap would have reinforced their efforts and helped sales.

Avon Products blundered in its approach to marketing cosmetics when it tried to employ housewives to sell door to door in their neighborhoods. What Avon didn't realize is that Japanese housewives are very hesitant to sell any products to people they don't know. The concept of inviting strangers into the home, like it is done in the West, is a completely unusual concept to Japanese women.

One fairly common U.S. practice is that of utilizing the same promotional strategy for all domestic subsidiaries. Promotional budgets often are based on a fixed-percentage-of-sales basis. This strategy often works well with domestic ventures but usually proves foolish when it is attempted for overseas subsidiaries as well. U.S. companies that try to force such standardization are often asking their foreign managers to do the impossible. For one thing, some types of media are not legally available. In many countries, no television advertisements are permitted. This alone makes a U.S.-style promotional budget infeasible. A second problem is one of scale. The use of a standard percentage of sales may be appropriate for large domestic subsidiaries, but for small foreign subsidiaries, 10 percent may not support a single promotional campaign. Several companies have attempted standardized promotional budgets, but most have now realized that each market provides different opportunities and challenges at different cost structures. A better strategy is to standardize the methods used to analyze opportunities and the methods used to develop local promotional budgets. Subsidiaries can then be urged to follow these established methods during the development of their own promotional budgets.

Cultural differences

Firms that failed to study local customs carefully have made dozens of blunders. As one example, consider the public display of physical contact between members of opposite sexes. In many countries, this is totally unacceptable and offensive. Thailand is one of these countries. A firm trying to introduce its mouthwash there, however, was not aware of this norm and promoted its product through an ad that displayed a young couple holding hands. By changing the advertisement to feature two women, the commercials were deemed acceptable and no longer offensive to the Thais.

The Asian Indians found a BiNoca Talc ad disturbing even though the woman in the advertisement was wearing a body stocking. The promotion, appearing in many of the major local newspapers, featured an attractive but apparently nude young woman lavishly splashing herself with BiNoca's talcum powder. Strategic portions of her body were carefully covered with the slogan "Don't go wild—just enough is all you need of BiNoca talc." The public, however, was not prepared for the ad's use of the female form and found the ads extremely indecent.

In other countries, such exposure is not deemed as offensive. In fact, the French, more than many nationalities, accept commercials that feature a great deal of the female body.

To some groups, the display of certain seemingly innocent parts of the body proves to be offensive. One U.S. shoe manufacturer promoted its product through photos of bare feet. Although considered a harmless advertisement by many, the photos were introduced in Southeast Asia where exposure of the foot is considered an insult.

Mountain Bell experienced a similar problem when one of its promotional photos depicted an executive talking on the telephone with his feet propped up on his desk. The photos, seen by Middle and Far Easterners, were considered to be in poor taste. To them, the display of the sole of the foot or shoe is a terrible insult.

Another U.S. firm trying to do business in Saudi Arabia ran into problems with some advertising artwork. The ad pictured a man's fist clenching a rock. This design was intended to symbolize the company's solid position as a manufacturer of rock-crushing equipment. Unfortunately, the upward position of the hand symbolized a motion considered very offensive by the Saudis. As pointed out previously, local input can be vital in avoiding blunders. Many promotional errors could have been averted had this warning been heeded.

Pepsodent reportedly tried to sell its toothpaste in regions of Southeast Asia through a promotion that stressed that the toothpaste helped enhance white teeth. In this area, where some local people deliberately chewed betel nut in order to achieve the social prestige of darkly stained teeth, such an ad was understandably less than effective. The slogan "You'll wonder where the yellow went" was also viewed by many as a racial slur.

A marketer of eyeglasses promoted his spectacles in Thailand using commercials that featured animals wearing glasses. This was an unfortunate decision, however, since animals there are considered a low life form, and it is beneath humans to wear anything worn by an animal.

The failure of firms to consider specialized aspects of local religions has created a number of difficulties. Companies have encountered problems in Asia when they incorporated pictures of Buddha in their promotions. Religious ties are strong in this area, and the use of local religious symbols in advertising is strongly resented —especially when words are deliberately or even accidentally printed across the picture of Buddha. One company was nearly burned to the ground when it ignorantly tried such a strategy. The seemingly minor incident led to a major international political conflict remembered for years.

Another religious-type blunder occurred when a refrigerator manufacturer ran an ad picturing a refrigerator containing a centrally placed chunk of ham. The typical refrigerator advertisement often features a refrigerator full of delicious food, and because these photos are difficult to take, the photos are generally used in as many places as possible. This company used its stock photo one place too many, though, when it was used in the Middle East where Muslims do not eat ham. Locals considered the ad to be both insensitive and unappealing.

An entertainment promoter also encountered difficulties when he failed to recognize one of the Muslim mores. He had booked Anita Sarawak in Singapore, and during her performance, encouraged her to hold her pet dog while singing "Me and you and a dog named Boo." This gimmick had worked well in other countries but caused a major commotion in Singapore. Plans for subsequent taped broadcasts of the show were cancelled, all because of the dog. According to Islamic beliefs, dogs are dirty and should not be shown or kept as pets.

Doubletree Hotels Corporation committed a costly blunder when it announced a national marketing campaign with a 30-second spot that was part of a $31 million campaign to convey employee personal warmth and quality of caring about the guests at the hotel. Instead, it found out from the Council on American–Islamic Relations, an Islamic advocacy group in Washington D.C., that the television ad was offensive. The ad portrayed three hotel employees dressed in Arab-style clothing bowing to guests. The complaint was that the employees appeared to be "praying" to guests, the way in which Muslims pray to God. This was interpreted as poking fun at another religion's prayer rituals. The Austin, Texas staff was completely unaware that the ad could be interpreted offensive to the Islamic community.

Saudi Arabia nearly restricted an airline from initiating flights when the company authorized "normal" newspaper advertisements. The ads featured attractive hostesses serving champagne to the happy airline passengers. Because in Saudi Arabia alcohol is illegal and unveiled women are not permitted to mix with men, the photo was viewed as an attempt to alter religious customs.

As stated earlier, successful advertisements usually involve cultural assumptions, so using the same commercial in more than one country can be dangerous. Cosmetics firms in the United States, for example, often pitch their messages to flatter the American woman's ego by telling her how attractive she is or will be if she uses their products. Similar commercials have been introduced in France and have failed. French women do not identify themselves as being ultra-glamorous nor do they believe that they can be. Often they do not even realize that the commercial is aimed at them, and so they simply assume that the message must be intended for a rare few.

Acceptable methods of information presentation also vary from culture to culture. In the Orient, for example, a person should not try to make the other "lose face." But to be taken seriously in Italy, a person must try to win the argument. A person speaking precisely will be taken literally in Switzerland. The British prefer a much "softer sell" than the Germans.

As mentioned previously, the choosing of a color is another important task. At least two different firms encountered problems in their Hong Kong marketing efforts when they decided to use green hats in commercials. One company attempted to sell its beer using the message that the beer was so good that even the Irish like it. The Irishman, of course, wore a green hat while drinking his beer. The other firm marketed cleaning agents and in its commercial featured individuals tossing hats at a male model. A green hat eventually landed on the man. In both cases, the color chosen was not appropriate; the green hat is a Chinese symbol used to identify a man as a cuckold. Understandably, both products were avoided.

As Guinness Stout can attest, Hong Kong has been the site of more than one unexpected turn of events. This firm's thick brew, considered especially well suited for the virile men of the British Empire, had somehow achieved a reputation in Hong Kong as being an excellent drink for women during pregnancy or menstrual periods. Consequently, when the drink was promoted in Hong Kong as one for men, it elicited much laughter. Any man ordering it was likely to be asked if it was his "time of the month!"

Another unusual problem occurred in Peru when a laundry detergent containing stain-removing enzymes was introduced through a cartoon depicting large-mouthed enzymes eating the dirt off of clothes. Although sales levels were initially good, they quickly dropped off. A local Peruvian custom was at the bottom of the company's problem. Peruvian women believed that they must boil their clothes to kill the germs, and the voracious cartoon creatures in the ad reinforced this belief. However, because the boiling destroyed the enzymes, the detergent did not perform as advertised.

As a result, since the product was not as effective as expected, the women only tried it once.

Not all companies find that their products are being used correctly, but sometimes unusual uses do not hurt sales. Gervais Danone, for example, was able to turn the tables on a potential problem. The company, finding that the Mexicans had little interest in its products, decided to alter its promotional strategy. It found that it was eventually able to interest the adults in using its cheeses for butter and its "Petite Suisse," a creamy whipped cheese, as a good snack for the children.

The Latin market in the United States

Not all cultural problems occur outside the multinational company's home country. For example, a significant Latin market exists in the United States, and it is becoming increasingly obvious that companies need to be aware of Latin culture. Sometimes it is even worth while to develop separate and special promotional campaigns aimed at this market. Colgate-Palmolive, for example, has been able to promote its toothpaste effectively within the Hispanic community through ads that place less emphasis on health and more emphasis on appearance. Not all companies are so successful, however. Several examples of misses or near misses in promotional efforts are cited in the following paragraphs.

Braniff Airlines produced one infamous advertisement that was broadcast in Spanish over several U.S. radio stations. Unfortunately, the speaker unintentionally encouraged travelers to "fly naked" when the message actually was intended to describe the leather seats in Braniff airplanes. Someone had written the message correctly, using "en cuero" for "in leather". But *en cueros* means "naked" in Spanish, and the "s" is not pronounced.

Therefore, both words sound the same. So while the message was technically correctly translated, had a native Spanish-speaking person looked over the ad first, the problem would not have arisen.

Coors commercials promoting the slogan "Taste the high country" featured people enjoying Coors beer and life in the Rocky Mountains. This approach, very effective with Anglo-Americans, did not appeal to Mexican-Americans, who could not identify with mountain life. Therefore, the Spanish language ads were modified. The mountains were identified as a good source of beer, but one did not necessarily need to live in the mountains to enjoy the beer or to be happy. The new slogan, in its English version, became "Take the beer from the high country and bring it to your high country—wherever it may be."

McDonald's has used "Hispanic ads" in several Spanish-speaking markets within the United States. However, these same ads proved unsuccessful when introduced into Puerto Rico. Apparently they were deemed as "too Mexican" so separate ads were developed.

In another McDonald's blunder that promoted Big Macs with a picture of a French master chef, the chef discovered that the publicity campaign was going on in the Netherlands. When the chef found out, he demanded $2.7 million in damages. The chef commented, "I have licensed my face and my name in all the countries of the world. This confusion between the art that we practice and the sandwich making they do cannot be tolerated." McDonald's settled with the chef, who donated the money to the Ecole des Arts Culinaires d'Ecully, where they train top-flight French chefs.

Johnson & Johnson was fortunate and discovered a potential cultural blunder in time to correct it. The firm was all set to promote its disposable diapers through advertisements that contained references to a mother's wet lap and a father's being dry when it was uncovered that such phrases bore indelicate sexual references to Hispanic consumers. This discovery was fortunate since such an ad would have created a great deal of embarrassment for the company.

Pedro Domecq wines also averted a mishap when it was about to use the slogan "the art of simpatico drinking" to promote Spanish wines. A U.S. advertising agency had created the slogan, which was intended to tie together the Spanish wine and the favorable U.S. translation and use of the word *simpatico*. However, the Spanish do not use the word with the same connotation. The correct Spanish usage is "El es muy simpatico" (he is very likable, agreeable, genial). Since, in Spanish, *simpatico* always refers to a person and never to drinking, the promotional campaign would have seemed foolish to the Spanish-speaking community. Fortunately, some Spanish-speaking managers from Pedro Domecq revealed this error in time.

Pricing

Setting an appropriate price for a product is often much more difficult than it appears. If only one insignificant detail of the pricing procedure is overlooked or misjudged, major troubles can develop for the firm.

Consider the experience of a company trying to market cans of luncheon meat. In order to beat the prices of its competitors, the firm slightly cut its prices by rounding them off to easy-to-record, even numbers. The customary prices of the competitors' products were a bit higher, and to the disappointment of the company, customers seemed quite willing to pay the minor extra charge. A local business practice was actually involved in this mishap. Local retail outlets usually operated on very small profit margins. These retailers found their customers would not request the small change owed when purchasing the fractionally higher priced can of meat. Naturally, in order to keep their "tip," the retailers heavily promoted the competition. It took the firm over six months to readjust its price and begin selling its product again.

The "Delacre" line of luxury biscuits promoted under the Pepperidge Farm label encountered problems when it was introduced into the United States. The biscuits did not sell well until the British firm Peek Frean introduced them at a much lower price. Products are not prized in all countries, so what some may be willing to pay highly for, others may not. In a foreign environment, any assumption concerning a product's "special value" is dangerous. Unless the market is clearly established, the implementation of a high pricing strategy is not likely to achieve high sales volumes.

Price negotiation can also prove to be a tricky undertaking. If the company negotiators are unaware of local customs, inappropriate prices are quite likely to result. This risk is best illustrated by examining the negotiation process involving Americans and Japanese. American managers are accustomed to pressure decision making and are often given the authority to make final decisions. Japanese managers, on the other hand, prefer to negotiate more slowly, tend to make decisions by group consensus, and always politely listen to everyone in their group before reaching an official decision. Because Americans are generally unaware of these tendencies, they have often created problems for themselves. A typical situation involves an American negotiating with Japanese managers in order to buy or sell some product or service. The American, often anxious to complete the deal, tends (in the eyes of the Japanese) to rush the negotiation process. All too often, when the time for price discussion arrives, the American will quickly suggest a price. Being used to the give-and-take of negotiating, the American usually does not make the best possible offer at the start nor necessarily expects it to be accepted. Here is where the troubles arise. When people hesitate, an American tends to assume that the price mentioned is an unacceptable one. Therefore, an American will sometimes hastily improve the offer even before it is rejected or the process is unsuccessfully terminated. But the American negotiating with Japanese managers may commit a blunder by quickly altering the price. This has happened on numerous occasions, but in at least one reported case, an American raised the price he was willing to pay three times after the Japanese were prepared to accept. Unaware of Japanese customs, he did not realize that the hesitation and discussion between the Japanese (in Japanese, of course) were not a result of unhappiness over the price quoted. With each higher price offer, the Japanese negotiators expressed amazement (in Japanese) but then proceeded to check out their colleagues' opinions. This delay only unwittingly encouraged the American to offer even more.

Many companies have been able to buy or sell merchandise at the right prices but have quoted the prices forgetting that exchange rates fluctuate. Because totally accurate exchange rate forecasting is not possible, some mistakes have been made. The direction of currency movement is fairly predictable, though, and should be considered when a company prices a contract for future payment.

Similarly, in most countries, inflation is fairly predictable. The failure to analyze inflationary factors has hurt a number of companies. A German company, for example, agreed to a $163 million Algerian construction contract. The price set was fair enough at the time of the commitment, but costs rose dramatically during the life of the contract. Unfortunately, the firm had failed to include protective price escalators in the original contract. Additionally, it soon discovered that payments were made in the local Algerian currency that had also declined in value. This double-edged sword cut out all the company's expected profits and cost the firm millions of dollars.

Credit, another price-related variable, is often critical to the marketing strategy. Although the product might be appropriately priced, it may not sell if credit terms are unacceptable. Consider a multinational firm that had carefully test-marketed its specially modified washing machines and concluded that they would sell well in Latin America. Sales were slow even though a large shipment had been made available. Eventually the firm discovered the trouble: local competitors were making their sales on credit. Apparently those participating in the market test had assumed that credit would be made available since it was the local business practice. So, when asked during the test if they would buy, they replied "yes." Only after they discovered that no credit would be provided did they change their minds and decide not to purchase the product. As evidenced, all aspects of pricing and selling strategies must be considered carefully.

SUMMARY

This chapter has introduced a number of problems encountered when companies attempted to promote products in international markets. Blunders have been made in all types of media and for a wide variety of reasons. Both simple and complex misunderstandings have led to difficulties. Sometimes mistakes arose from human error or the use of culturally insensitive persons. On occasion, an entire promotional strategy has proved foolish. In many cases, the blunders were simply the result of the company's failure to understand cultural differences, some basic but some more subtle. A few problems encountered were based upon pricing errors. With so many different kinds of potential blunders, it is easy to believe that every promotional task imaginable has been bungled at one time or another by someone, someplace.

CHAPTER 5

Translation

- Carelessness
- Multiple Meanings
- Idioms
- Summary

Translation

Translation errors are the cause of the greatest number and variety of blunders in international business. There are three basic categories of translation errors: simple carelessness, multiple-meaning words, and idioms. All three types are described and discussed in this chapter.

Carelessness

The most prevalent type of translation blunder is merely the careless rendering of a promotional message into another language. Obviously, these mistakes can often result in an embarrassing or damaging situation and thus directly injure sales.

Consider the case of the Doutor Coffee Company, a Tokyo retailer. It was trying to promote coffee as relaxing and wanted to convey "it takes a load off your chest." But the phrase came out as "ease your bosoms," a rough translation of the English slogan.

A food company did indeed make a "big mistake" when it advertised its giant burrito as a "burrada." The colloquial meaning of the word *burrada is* "big mistake." Spanish language translations seem to be treacherous for some companies. One Spanish ad promoted Budweiser as the "Queen of Beers"—just a bit off their usual "King of Beers" slogan. Another Spanish-language blunder was made when an advertisement for "Bud Lite" beer was translated into Spanish as "Filling, less delicious" rather than "Delicious, less filling."

In an advertisement that ran in New York, Acura proudly proclaimed, "The Legend and Integra, cars that break tradition, *now* your bank account." Obviously Acura intended to say "not" rather than "now," but to some consumers the error may have an accidental ring of truth to it.

An American in Michigan got so upset with the success of Japanese auto makers that he decided to make and sell T-shirts displaying a message that was supposed to say in both English and Japanese "Buy American made". Naturally, he had no trouble with the English, but the Japanese translation came out as "Buy an American maid." Close!

A toy bear, made in Taiwan, "sang" Christmas carols in English. One song, though, didn't quite come out correctly: it was "Oh, little town of Birmingham." It helps to know the story!

One company in Taiwan tried to sell diet food to expatriates living there. The company urged consumers to buy its product to add "roughage" to their systems. How much "roughage" should a person consume? Well, the instructions claimed that one should eat it until "your tool floats." Do you suppose they meant "stool?"

An automobile manufacturer promoted its product in an English-speaking market by declaring that its product "topped them all." This may have been so, but the French Canadians would not have known. When the product was introduced, the phrase was mistranslated in French. The result: the company actually boasted that its cars were "topped by them all." Another U.S. manufacturer in the auto industry advertised its auto battery as "highly rated." Unfortunately, when the company introduced its product in Venezuela, the battery was described as "highly overrated." Here again the company had used a thoughtless translation of a key promotional phrase. Needless to say, sales did not boom in either case.

Translation blunders are easy to make—especially if you are speaking in a difficult language you do not have experience in. Finnish is widely recognized as a difficult language, but some organizations try to bring their messages to Finland in Finnish anyway. Usually, it is worth while, but every so often the results have been "awkward." The Church of Jesus Christ of Latter-day Saints (the "Mormon Church") is one of the organizations that has had some problems in Finland. It regularly sends some of its members there to learn Finnish and talk with the people about the Church. These missionaries are so well intended and sincere-sounding, however, that it is usually quite amusing to the local Finnish listener to hear the missionary say, "We are American missionaries and we go around killing people." Apparently this happens frequently because the Finnish word for "meeting" is *tappamaan*, but that word is often mispronounced by foreigners as "tapamaan," which means "killing".

Kentucky Fried Chicken has done very well overseas, as many can attest. However, even a good company can make mistakes. KFC experienced real problems when the phrase "finger lickin' good" came out in Chinese as "eat your fingers off." Eastern Airlines translated its "We earn our wings daily" message into Spanish in such a way that the translated message implied that the airline's passengers often ended up dead. This, naturally, did not help Eastern's struggle to avoid bankruptcy. And the Olfa Corporation, a Japanese manufacturer, sold knives in the United States with a very interesting warning on the package, "Caution: blade extremely sharp! Keep out of children."

A Canadian importer of Turkish shirts destined for Quebec used a dictionary to help him translate the label "Made in Turkey". Unfortunately, his translated message, "Fabriqué en Dinde," reflected his knowledge of French—*dinde* is the bird, Turquie is the country.

Some years ago, the prestigious prep school, Phillips-Exeter, established its own "School Year Abroad" (SYA) program in Barcelona, Spain. As Thanksgiving rolled around, the director called in his young, bilingual, Spanish secretary and instructed her to get a half-dozen turkeys for this important American holiday. She immediately called the Turkish Consulate General. Not much was going on, so they were thrilled to accept the invitation. Still on the phone, the secretary informed the director of SYA that she had the six Turkeys and asked how they should come dressed. The director replied, "Make sure they're *cleaned.*"

An interesting, but unimpressive, warning label was displayed on the irons made by the German company Rowenta. It said, "Do not iron clothes on body." The label did not inspire confidence in the product or its manufacturer.

Careless translations can prove to be humorous to the consumer and/or embarrassing to the firm. Consider, for example, the experience of the Otis Engineering Corporation when it participated in an exhibition held in Moscow. Initially, the company's representatives could not discern why its display won Soviet snickers as well as praise. Much to their disappointment and embarrassment, it was discovered that a careless translator had rendered a sign that identified "completion equipment" as "equipment for orgasms."

On the opposite side of the globe, another firm was experiencing the headaches caused by a poor translator. In this case, a Mexican magazine promotion for an American-brand shirt carried a message stating the exact opposite of what had originally been intended. The advertisement, instead of declaring "When I used this shirt, I felt good," read "Until I used this shirt, I felt good."

There is an old saying, "The world is paved with good intentions." This certainly holds true for many international business endeavours. However, effort alone just is not enough sometimes. This might be best illustrated with the experiences of one Japanese firm trying to do business in China. In order to present itself in a better light, it decided to have English-language labels on its products. It thought this would add prestige to its products, but the Japanese messages were so poorly translated into English that the results were quite negative. After all, who would be interested in meat called "liver putty," a toilet paper named "My Fanny Brand," ready-to-eat pancakes identified as "strawberry crap dessert"; an antifreeze spray claimed to be a "hot piss brand," or a health product that was recommended by a pediatrician (doctor for children) who was called a "specialist in *deceased* children"?

Public signs translated from foreign languages and designed to assist English-speaking visitors are sources of lost meaning in the translation. In Zurich the notice said, "Because of the impropriety of entertaining guests of the opposite sex in the bedroom, it is suggested that the lobby be used for this purpose." In an Acapulco hotel when trying to promote quality control, "the manager has personally passed all the water served here."

International business people often encounter some interesting signs in their hotels while travelling abroad. Try to guess where these were found:

"Please leave your values at the front desk" (Paris).

"The flattening of underwear with pleasure is the job of the chambermaid" (Zagreb).

"The lift is being fixed for the next day. During that time we regret that you will be unbearable" (Bucharest).

Of course people have poorly translated English into other languages as well. "Violators will be fined" was translated into Spanish to say, "Rapists will be killed" (Phoenix). Posters and advertisements were also printed in Phoenix which were supposed to say "Hear the concert of the year" in Spanish, but the curly tilde over the letter "n" in one word was omitted. This resulted in the message actually saying, "Hear the concert of the anus." It is not clear how many people attended this concert.

A sign in a cocktail lounge in Norway read "Ladies are requested not to have children at the bar." In Moscow a sign in a hotel welcomes you to "visit the cemetery where famous Russian and Soviet composers, artists and writers are buried daily except Thursday." Participants at a conference must have smiled when they read a sign which said, "For anyone who has children and doesn't know it, there is a day care on the first floor."

The zoo in Budapest tells visitors, "Please do not feed the animals. If you have any suitable food, give it to the guard on duty." An airline office in Copenhagen promises to "take your bags and send them in all directions." Some clothing signs advertised more than they bargained for when they said, "fur coats made for ladies from their own skin." Even the dry cleaners' ads may convey some peculiar offerings such as "Drop your trousers here for best results" in Bangkok or "Ladies, leave your clothes here and spend the afternoon having a good time" in Rome.

Restaurants seem to have the same kind of loss in translation problems. A Polish menu advertised "roasted duck let loose" while a Swiss diner sent a warning message, "Our wines leave you nothing to hope for," and a bathroom sign in Finland suggests, "To stop the drip, turn cock to right."

The Frank Perdue Company is well known for its catchy messages promoting its chicken products. At least one of its popular slogans, though, was not translated very well. The message, declaring approximately "It takes a tough man to make a tender chicken," somehow came out closer to "It takes a sexually excited man to make a chick affectionate."

Many a small business has thwarted its own efforts through the use of poor translation. For example, one businessperson, trying to save a bit of money, hired an Indonesian exchange student to translate the instruction manual of a computer destined for Jakarta. Not surprisingly, the student did not understand computer terminology, so the computer "software" was translated as "underwear." The manual must have provided interesting reading!

In efforts to attract tourists and foreign business people, some small businesses have created rather funny situations. For instance, public signs translated from foreign languages, and designed to assist English-speaking visitors, are sometimes sources of confusion in the translation. A department store in Thailand posted a sign that read "Visit our bargain basement one flight up." Another misguided individual in Thailand tried to attract business with a sign that asked, "Would you like to ride on your ass?" And in Japan, an interesting but misleading translation showed up on a sign in a Japanese garden. The posted sign read, "Japanese garden is the mental home of the Japanese."

English translations around the world carry lost meanings in translation. In a Belgrade hotel elevator: "To move the cabin, push button for wishing floor. If the cabin should enter more persons, each one should press a number of wishing floor. Driving is then going alphabetically by national order." A hotel in Athens wants visitors to "complain at the office between the hours of 9 a.m. and 11 a.m. daily." In Tokyo at the bar you can order "special cocktails for the ladies with nuts."

A car rental firm in Tokyo printed a brochure to assist drivers that read, "When passenger of foot heave in sight, tootle the horn. Trumpet him melodiously at first, but if he still obstacles your passage then tootle him with vigor." Or in a Leipzig elevator the sign read, "Do not enter lift backwards, and only when lit up."

The frequency of these sorts of amusing translations is amazing. In an Austrian ski resort hotel, guests were told "Not to perambulate the corridors in the hours of repose in the boots of ascension." Two different signs above a shop entrance convincingly state "English well talking" and "Here speeching American." In Akko, Israel, a restaurant featured "lamp chops". In a Polish hotel the menu offers "Salad a firm's own make: limpid red beet soup with cheesy dumplings in the form of a finger; roasted duck let loose; and beef rashers beaten up in the country people's fashion."

In fact, menus seem to be the most interesting place to find these entertaining translations. They seem to be everywhere. A restaurant in China offered "cold shredded children" and "dreaded veal cutlet." A restaurant in Vietnam offered "pork with fresh garbage," while one in Los Angeles offered "French creeps." It is possible, of course, that these menus were not printed in error at all, but one hopes so.

A number of years ago U.S. businessmen reported seeing a sign in a Tokyo hotel which read "You are respectfully requested to take advantage of the chambermaids." The translation is probably misleading, but not as costly as the faulty translations of some equipment-handling instructions that have led to the injury and death of several construction employees in the Middle East.

An interesting sign in Czechoslovakia read, "Take one of our horse-driven tours. We guarantee no miscarriages." That, however, probably didn't generate as much interest as the sign in a French shop window that read, "We sell dresses for street walking." It is probably best to assume that both signs were the result of translation errors.

One dentist in Hong Kong apparently advertises "Teeth extracted by the latest Methodists." A more startling sign, however, showed up in the window of a tailor in Jordan. The sign advised: "Order you summers suit. Because if big rush we will execute customers in strict rotation."

A company in Taiwan wished to help foreigners communicate more effectively, so it advertised its expertise in a brochure. The text read, in part, that "communication was a new challenge," and that the firm could "translet [sic] your idea clearly . . . to people who have no lot of time to sit or listen." Obviously, the firm needed to hire someone to help it improve its own communication skills!

A Chinese restaurant in Virginia ran an ad in a local newspaper with a line of Chinese characters printed upside down. That is an understandable mistake, but the restaurant compounded this mistake in its subsequent ad that tried to explain the error. The characters were the correct way up in the second ad, but in reverse order. There is no report as to how the third version looked.

A firm in the Middle East was able to attract attention, but not exactly the kind it had hoped. It seems that a Saudi Arabian laundry had posted, in English, a list of its cleaning prices. It was not its prices, though, that were attracting people. The company had used a poor translator, and among the many spelling errors on the poster was the omission of the letter "r" in lady's shirt." One can imagine the customers' reactions! It is easy to understand the importance of an accurate translation and the negative results possible if this work is not done carefully.

One of the more unusual errors made by a small business occurred in Kowloon. A sign in the hotel read, "It is forbidden to steal hotel towels, please if you are not person to do such is please not to read notice." What one can assume from this is that someone tried to communicate in another language, but with a bit of difficulty.

Poorly translated signs in business windows and establishments seem to be very common. In fact, as of this writing, a well established and frequently updated website is reporting hundreds of recently discovered incidents—each documented with photos of the frequently humorous blunders. (Some sections of the website may be offensive or at least too graphic for some people, but these sections can easily be avoided.) For more information, go to www.engrish.com.

Translation blunders seem to occur everywhere but for now consider only one area of the world—Quebec. Quebec has been the site of a number of corporate blunders, most of them due to simple carelessness. There is no reason, for example, for a firm to have used the words *lavement d'auto* (car enema) instead of the correct *lavage d'auto* (car wash), but one firm did. Another company boasted of "lait frais usage" (used fresh milk) when it meant to brag of "lait frais employé" (fresh milk used). The "terrific" pens of one firm were promoted as "terrifiantes" (terrifying) instead. Indeed, such a poor translation is terrifying! One company, intending to report that its appliance would use any kind of electrical current, actually stated that the appliance wore out any kind of liquid. And imagine how one company felt when its product to reduce heartburn was advertised as one that reduced warmth of heart. Another unfortunate firm claimed that its product was a stumbling block to success when it really wanted to claim that its product provided a stepping stone to success.

The omission of an accent mark created difficulties for at least one company. An American firm hoped to surprise its Mexican-based employees with a New Year's Eve party. Preparations were complete, including balloons with printed slogans (in Spanish) declaring "Happy New Year." However, the tilde accent mark over the "n" in *año* was left off. Without the mark, the word read "ano" ("anus" in Spanish). Happy New Anus? Needless to say, the balloons came down before midnight!

All of these blunders point out that even the smallest translation error can greatly affect the intended message and the market's reaction to that message. Occasionally it may only be one seemingly insignificant letter that can change the entire context of the copy. Consider one unfortunate international corporation that had its annual report translated into Spanish. In the sentence "Our vast enterprise achieved record sales . . ." the word "vast" was translated into *basto*. The actual Spanish word is *vasto*, but people often become confused because the letters "b" and "v" are pronounced similarly. Due to this error in translation, however, the entire meaning of the sentence was modified to "our crude and uncultured enterprise achieved record sales . . ."

Poor translations get companies into trouble more often than anything else. Usually, these translations are only embarrassing, but sometimes they can be much more serious. Mead Johnson Nutritionals found this out the hard way. It had to recall two different baby food products because the instructions on how the products were to be prepared had been incorrectly translated from English to Spanish. Both the 16 oz powder infant formula and the 32 oz ready-to-use infant formula had dangerous preparation instructions, according to the U.S.

Food and Drug Administration. It reported that, if the baby food were prepared according to the incorrect Spanish instructions, the formula could cause seizures, irregular heartbeat, renal failure and death. Obviously, no company wants to make this kind of blunder.

While selling products in Mexico, Microsoft Corporation committed a blunder when the Word 6.0 program suggested a series of synonyms in the thesaurus that were offensive. Examples included words such as "man-eater," "cannibal" or "barbarian" that were replaced by the Spanish term for black people. The thesaurus recommended in place of "indians" to use the term "man-eating savages." The term "lesbian" suggested substituting the word "vicious" or "perverse." "Occidental" was more positively portrayed, with synonyms such as "white," "civilized" and "cultured."

Multiple Meanings

The second category of translation blunders involves translated messages that can convey more than one meaning. The trials and tribulations experienced by the Parker Pen Company serve as an excellent illustration of how an innocent translation of a multiple-meaning word or phrase can create complex problems. In its advertisements destined for Latin America, Parker had hoped to use the word *bola* to describe its ballpoint pen. However, it was discovered that the word conveys different meanings in different Latin countries. To some, *bola* conveys the intended meaning of "ball," while in another country, the translation means "revolution." *Bola* represents an obscenity in a third country, and in yet another, it means a "lie" or "fabrication." Luckily, the firm was able to uncover this translation problem before it could ever become a blunder.

The company, however, was not so fortunate when it tried to introduce its fountain pens in some parts of Latin America. The Parker Pen Company had developed and promoted in the United States one of the first truly reliable fountain pens. The pen could be carried in a person's shirt without the person worrying about the possibility of embarrassing ink stains. The advertisements (and the pens) performed so well that the Parker pen became quite well known. Eventually, the promotion was shortened to convey that Parker pens avoid embarrassment. Because this condensed version of the promotional slogan was so successful over time, the older expanded message was taken for granted and basically forgotten. Later, when the firm decided to enter the Latin American market, it merely translated the same condensed promotional slogan then being used in the United States: "Avoid embarrassment—use Parker pens." The company even posted metal signs featuring this short message on the buildings in which its pens were sold, but the results of the company's promotional efforts were not as anticipated. What had gone wrong? The company had promoted a slogan that contained a multiple-meaning word. The Spanish word for "embarrassment" was also used to indicate pregnancy, so the Parker Pen Company was unknowingly promoting its pens as contraceptives![1]

An American toothpaste manufacturer also experienced pains with its "pregnancy." The company promised its customers that they would be more "interesting" if they used the firm's toothpaste. What the advertising coordinators did not realize, however, was that in some Latin American countries "interesting" is another euphemism for "pregnant."

Continuing with problems of pregnancy, consider the case of a freelance Arabic translator who translated an American computer manual into his native language.

When confronted with the terms "dummy" and "load," specialized electronics terms, he consulted his dictionary and found the equivalents of "dummy" and "load." When he put these two together, he produced the Arabic term for "false pregnancy."

The Dairy Association's huge success with the campaign "Got milk?" prompted them to expand advertising to Mexico. However, it was soon brought to their attention that the Spanish translation read "Are you lactating?"

A clothing store in Tokyo claimed that "Our nylons cost more than common, but you'll find they are the best in the long run."

Wendy's was saved from committing two separate blunders in Germany by advertising agency staff members. In one case, Wendy's wanted to promote its "old-fashioned" qualities. A literal translation, however, would have resulted in the company promoting itself as "outdated". In another example, Wendy's wanted to emphasize that its hamburgers could be prepared 256 ways. The problem? The German word Wendy's wanted to use for "ways" usually meant "roads" or "highways." Although such errors may sometimes entertain the public, it is certainly preferable to catch these mistakes before they confuse the consumer or embarrass the company.

The Spanish certainly enjoyed a good laugh when Chrysler Corporation tried to promote its successful U.S. slogan, "Dart is power." It seems that the translated version of this message implied that drivers of the car needed sexual vigor!

The well-known vacuum cleaner manufacturer, Electrolux, is a Swedish-owned company. New ads were developed for the U.S. market proclaiming "Electrolux sucks better." Obviously, the firm was not attuned to some common American slang! In Thailand, a bar located nearby some trees and buildings that blocked out the hot sun innocently advertised itself as "the shadiest bar in Bangkok."

These double-meaning translation errors embarrass the firms involved. One company caught in this situation was granted the dubious distinction of winning *Playboy* magazine's annual "Booby-Boo-Boo Award." Apparently when Hunt-Wesson introduced the "Big John" family brand in Canada it experienced a bit of difficulty with the French translation. The name, translated as "Gros Jos," also turned out to be a colloquial French expression that denoted a woman with large breasts. In this case the company was fortunate. Its sales were not badly hurt, for a number of men wanted to order the "Gros Jos"!

Hunt-Wesson has not been the only company to find itself in such a humorous position. A U.S. airline that proudly advertised swank "rendezvous lounges" aboard its Boeing 747 jets may have wished that its promotion had never reached Brazil. After advertising these accommodations, the company belatedly learned that "rendezvous" in Portuguese represents a room that is rented out for prostitution. Although the promotion was successful in attracting attention, sales did not increase. No Brazilian wanted to be seen getting on or off the airline's plane. Here again a company's failure to understand all of the meanings and implications of the translated message was responsible for its subsequent difficulties.

Several major tobacco companies have also experienced the pitfall of a double meaning. These firms advertised "low-tar" cigarettes in Spanish-speaking countries but misused the word *brea*. *Brea* literally translates to "tar," but it is the type of tar used for paving streets. Care for a "low-asphalt" cigarette, anyone?

A sign in a Japanese museum advised patrons in English to "Please refrain from taking photographs and reproducing." Literal translations are risky. It is probably just as well that most people in English-speaking countries do not know that the motto of Tokyo Gas & Electric is "My life, my gas."

Translated words may often mean about the same thing, but they may not elicit the same feelings. As an example, "As smooth as a baby's bottom" was translated into Japanese to "As smooth as a baby's ass." Translators must be encouraged to convey the intended mood even if this means that they must forgo a literal translation and use some alternative wording instead.

American cooks understand what is meant by tomato "paste", but how does one translate this into Arabic? The closest translation is something like "tomato glue." Thus, translators have had to use the Arabic words for "tomato puree." Sounds a bit more appetizing, doesn't it?

Sometimes someone in a company simply forgets that words have well-known double meanings. One firm, for example, experienced trouble conducting market research. It requested information regarding the annual German production of washers. The firm was actually seeking data on washing machines but, instead, received material on the production of flat metal discs (also known as washers). Here the translation problem was not so much with the translated word or the translator but with the original word.

Adolph Coors Company hired an agency to develop promotional material for its Coors Light beer that would appeal to Hispanics in the United States. The copywriter tried to translate the phrase "Turn it loose" into Spanish, but unfortunately used words which meant "Drink Coors and get diarrhea." The commercial received a lot of attention but not the kind Coors had hoped for!

Tropicana tried to sell its orange juice in Miami, claiming that it was "jugo de China." "China" means "orange" to Puerto Ricans, but not to the Cubans in Miami. Thus, the Cubans thought that it was "juice from China" and were not very interested in the product.

Miami is frequently the location for linguistic problems. Several different cultures coexist there, with people speaking different languages—or sometimes the same one with different meanings. Take the word *bichos*, for example. It means "bugs" to Mexicans, but the word denotes a man's private parts to Puerto Ricans. Therefore, the insecticide company's posters guaranteeing that its products would kill all "bichos" was not very successful in some parts of Miami!

One final example of the troublesome multiple-meaning word involves the banking industry. An American bank was given a 30-day option on the purchase of a Middle Eastern bank. During the final negotiations, an unfortunate buyer proposed in French that the loans be put into an escrow account. The local sellers, quite humiliated and shocked, quickly left the room shouting, "A reserve for cheating? Never!" The misunderstanding stemmed from the word *escrow* which when translated into French means a cheat. Quite upset, the sellers decided to find another interested party willing to purchase the bank.

Translations play a key role in all aspects of international business, and accuracy is of utmost importance. A company can be hurt greatly by one simple faulty translation.

Idioms

Having discussed not only those errors resulting from careless translation but also those due to multiple meanings, consider now the third type of blunder: those made during the translation of idioms and expressions. Because of the unique aspect of the idiomatic expressions that characterize every language, this is often the most difficult area. The following examples have been chosen as illustrations.

Most firms realize it takes more than a bilingual dictionary to translate commercial messages and their intended meanings. However, a few firms have used the simplest, most literal translations for their promotions and as a result have found themselves promoting something other than what they had thought. An American company, for instance, advertised its product to a Spanish audience, exclaiming that anyone who didn't wear its brand of hosiery just "wouldn't have a leg to stand on." But when the copy was translated the firm actually declared that the wearer would "only have one leg."

Another case of a troublesome literal translation occurred in French-speaking Quebec. The point-of-sale campaign of a laundry soap company stressed the extra-strong cleaning powers of its product and how great it was for the especially dirty parts of the wash, "les parts de sale." When the soap sales declined, the company investigated and discovered that this phrase is comparable to the American slang phrase "private parts."

The American expression "touch-toe" was responsible for a blunder made by a manufacturer of dental equipment. In a brochure written for the Soviet market, the company featured the "touch-toe" control of its dental chair movement. The translator, however, rendered the description of this feature in such a way that the Russians thought that the dentist had to be barefooted in order to operate the equipment. What a unique feature, indeed!

Several other brief examples of mistranslated English idioms or expressions can be cited to illustrate how often these blunders have been made. One European firm certainly missed the point when it translated the expression "out of sight, out of mind" as "invisible things are insane" in Thailand. There is also the story of the phrase "the spirit is willing, but the flesh is weak" being translated to "the liquor is holding out all right, but the meat has spoiled." And consider, finally, a translation of "Schweppes Tonic Water" to the Italian *il water*. The copy was speedily dehydrated to "Schweppes Tonica" because *il water* idiomatically indicates a bathroom.

If anything is to be learned from these examples, it is the necessity for caution in the translation and interpretation of intended messages. Exact wording should not always be translated literally. This can be most appropriately demonstrated by citing ten idioms used in the United States. If any of these were to be used in Quebec, for example, the French translation should not be a literal one but should approximate the local phrase or idiom commonly used there. The U.S. version is mentioned first and is followed by the comparable French Canadian expression.

"To murder the King's English" should be translated as "to speak French like a Spanish cow."

"Nothing to sneeze at" should become "nothing to spit on."

"Welcome as a bull in a china shop" should become "welcome as a dog in a bowling alley."

"A little birdie told me so" should become "my little finger told it to me."

"To be sitting on the fence" should become "to swim between two streams."

"I have a hangover" should become "I have a sore hair."

"To cry in one's beer" should become "to have the sad wine."

"Unable to make head or tail of it" should become "to lose one's Latin."

"To make a mountain out of a molehill" should become "to drown in a glass of water."

"You can't teach an old dog new tricks" should become "one does not teach an old monkey to make faces."[2]

It need not be an entire phrase that needs rewording, but only one simple word. What the people of one country take for granted as the only correct word or sound might be totally inappropriate to others. Take, for example, the words used for animal sounds. In reality, an animal makes the same noise in every country, but humans interpret the sound differently from country to country. Companies that sell pet food and supplies and those taking the risky approach of featuring animals in promotions need to take extra precautions when speaking for animals. If the messages are to be effective, then the firms must be sure that they are communicating in languages that can be understood.

SUMMARY

Faulty translations have caused the most blunders in international business. These translation mistakes have hindered not only marketing efforts and negotiations but also many other aspects of business. They are usually due to carelessness, but language subtleties, words with multiple meanings, and difficult-to-translate idioms also cause problems.

Fortunately, translation blunders are some of the easiest to avoid. Methods to avoid these errors are discussed in Chapter 9.

CHAPTER 6

Management

- Cultural Differences
- Poor Personnel Choices
- Labor Relations
- Summary

Management

"Management"—the act, manner, or practice of managing, handling, or controlling something. Certainly a dictionary's basic definition of this word helps us understand why so many blunders can occur in this area of business.

An American executive's mishandling of a presentation prepared for a small Caribbean country serves as a simple example of a management blunder. The meeting was held in the Prime Minister's conference room, and the executive began his presentation with, "Honorable Mr. Tollis and esteemed members of the cabinet." The Prime Minister interrupted him several times, asking him to start over. Eventually, someone advised the bewildered and then embarrassed businessman that Mr. Tollis had been deposed six months earlier!

Unfortunately, people sometimes get careless. Thoughtless conversations, however, can prove costly. When in a foreign-speaking country, it is easy to forget that some people may understand many languages. All too often, speakers learn too late that others understand what they are saying. In fact, visitors to the United States often assume no one understands their native tongue and then promptly say something they quickly regret. An Italian businessman, for example, reportedly flew to Los Angeles to talk with a potential American investor.

The driver of the American picked up the Italian at the airport. Believing that the driver did not understand Italian, the visitor, speaking in Italian, apparently made some very negative remarks about the potential investor to his accompanying business associate. These remarks were reported by the driver, who did indeed understand what was being said, and the business deal collapsed.

There are many facets of management. Consider Renault, which, like many firms, has tried to use various barter plans but has experienced mixed success. Trading cars for other products can be profitable but only if the traded products are correctly marketed. In order to sell its cars in South America, Renault agreed to accept coffee beans in payment. The plan seemed safe, as coffee beans are easily traded on world commodity markets. Renault's problems began when the company decided to use the beans to produce instant coffee rather than simply sell the coffee beans wholesale. Without carefully checking the credentials of a fast-talking businessman, Renault agreed to build two plants employing his "miracle new process" for the production of instant coffee. Renault later learned that its new associate had earlier run into legal problems with some of his other international business schemes, but not before it discovered that the "miracle process" failed to work properly and that its new associate had disappeared. Renault lost about $120 million but learned a valuable lesson.

Imperial-Eastman Corporation encountered numerous problems in the operations of its various overseas enterprises. In at least one instance, the company experienced unexpected difficulties when it failed to retain its overseas U.S. personnel for a long enough period of time. Before the operation's critical start-up period was completely over, the company relieved its U.S. personnel and relied solely on its locally hired staff to continue running the operation. However, as critical problems developed, Imperial-Eastman discovered that the local staff was not sufficiently experienced to handle the difficult problems resulting from the new operation. In other ventures, the company suffered from poor estimates of initial inventory needs that created production/delivery disruptions. Losses were incurred when the firm did not allow for delayed delivery and subcontractors failed to deliver on time.

A precarious balance seems to exist between the number of foreign managers and the number of U.S. managers needed for a successful operation. Imperial-Eastman experienced problems by relying too heavily on inexperienced local managers, but General Electric encountered troubles by its placement and retention of U.S. employees in most managerial positions. In some cases, because the U.S. employees were unfamiliar with the local business practices, they unknowingly nullified the firm's ability to compete with local business people.

General Electric encountered more culturally oriented management problems in France. Its French employees were upset when they were ordered to wear GE T-shirts to a function (too American), post English-language posters, and in general behave as if the subsidiary was an extension of the United States. Eventually, compromises were made on both sides, but morale already had been badly damaged.

The cases cited above are typical of the types of management blunders that have plagued multinational corporations. Management problems are most often caused by cultural differences that outside managers do not understand and by labor practices with which they are unfamiliar.

Cultural Differences

A Korean firm, Kunja Industrial Company, which owns the Kunja Knitting Mills plant in South Carolina, made the news when an American employee innocently "crooked" his "pointing finger" trying to catch the attention of his Korean boss and bring him closer. The employee succeeded in getting attention all right. However, he certainly didn't succeed in getting his boss physically or emotionally any closer. In fact, he was almost fired. The U.S. finger-moving gesture for asking someone to come closer is considered a vulgar gesture in Korea!

A similar blunder was made by former President George Bush. The President was visiting Australia. As he walked up the stairs to his plane, he turned and gave a thumbs up signal, thinking he was indicating that things had gone well. Perhaps they had—at least to that point —but the thumbs-up gesture in Australia is essentially the equivalent of the raised middle finger in the United States. Unknowingly, he had correctly indicated that things ended badly.

Culture includes how different people dress and what is considered acceptable business attire. A notable blunder occurred when Spanish businessmen arrived in Saudi Arabia with a full delegation, confident that they had prepared to encourage the Saudis to spend some of their oil money on Spanish products. The entourage included a number of young, intelligent, bilingual (Spanish/English) women dressed in the height of current style. The blunder occurred when the Saudi police took one look at the miniskirts of the female delegates and immediately shipped the entire group home on the next plane to Spain. Traditionally, women do not show their bare legs in Saudi Arabian culture.

When doing business in another country, it is often easy to assume that things there are the same as in your country. Sometimes they are, but sometimes they are different. One U.S. firm with a subsidiary in a small island state learned this the hard way when it hired a local manager to run the subsidiary. One person was highly recommended by local contacts, was intelligent, well spoken, and related well to the local workers. She was interviewed by a representative from headquarters and seemed to be the best choice for the position. Initially, operations seemed to go quite well, but it soon became evident that there was a problem. Major discrepancies surfaced in terms of inventory levels and in the reports of parts shipped. The cause of these problems was finally uncovered. The manager could not do the basic arithmetic of adding or subtracting—skills critical to the job. No one had thought to ask about these skills because they were simply assumed.

It is also wise to know the proper way to dismiss an employee when working with other cultures. This is a difficult task to perform in familiar territory but it is especially tricky when one is in a foreign country and does not always fully understand the local culture. An American manager stationed in Indonesia reportedly discovered this when he tried to fire an oilrig employee. Rather than notifying the employee privately of his dismissal, the manager publicly told the timekeeper to send the man "packing." In Indonesia, this public dismissal was considered an unacceptable "loss of face" which offended both the dismissed man and his friends. So, rather than leave quietly, the man grabbed fire axes and ran after the American manager. Reportedly, the American was barely rescued in time. Obviously, it is dangerous to ignore local management practices and customs!

In an attempt to offer U.S. Southern hospitality, an American businessman was saying goodbye to a

Saudi Arabian businessman at the airport after a successful meeting and finished with, "Y'all come and visit." Apparently the Saudi businessman was mortally offended because it was inconceivable to the Saudi that he and his chauffeur should be invited to the United States.

Another American manager was sent to Malaysia to close a major deal. While there he was introduced to someone he thought was named Roger so he proceeded to call him "Rog" several times during the negotiations. Unfortunately, this important potential client was a "rajah," which is an important Malaysian title of nobility. The U.S. tendency to use first names, and even more familiar abbreviated names, was the cause of a serious error in this case. Rather than showing respect, the American appeared disrespectful and insensitive. When the error was discovered, the damage had been done. It is always best to know whom you are dealing with in advance and how that person prefers to be addressed.

A Brazilian executive created major problems for his firm when he treated his secretaries in the United States as personal servants. Not only did he ask them to do his personal shopping, he even asked them to mend his clothes!

The acquisition of the Firestone tire company by Japan's Bridgestone did not proceed as smoothly as hoped. In fact, John Nevin, a crusty former chairman of Firestone, admitted that his style appeared abrupt and abrasive at times to the Japanese, whose manner is much more subtle. He needed to be less direct and forceful with them and they had to become more aware of American-style directness. Both sides tried to adjust, but it did not work out, so new managers had to be brought in.

Milwaukee-based Manpower chairman, Mitchell Fromstein, reports that Blue Arrow, a British employment firm, took over Manpower in 1987 but put little effort into understanding how the U.S. labor market differed from the British market. Even the company newsletter directed to the U.S. market ignored U.S. interests. American managers began to openly rebel. Eventually, the Americans wound up in control of the combined company.

In Las Vegas, the Japanese owners of the casinos reportedly ran into problems when they tried to use Japanese management techniques. Among other things, they tried to make decisions the typical Japanese way—by consensus. The approach works well in Japan for many firms but was deemed as too slow and cumbersome in the fast-moving casino environment.

An American company went to a great deal of expense to carefully plan a massive layoff of employees in one of its European subsidiaries. Just before the plan was implemented, however, the firm learned that such layoffs were illegal. Time and money could easily have been saved had managers known of the local labor laws.

In a wave of ethnocentrism the new American owners of a Spanish company changed the firm's previous prestigious Spanish name to that of the U.S. parent, flew the American flag from the company flagpole, and widely announced the sophisticated and superb technology being introduced. The company even suggested that those who had managed the company prior to the takeover by the Americans were incompetent. Then, in a special interview with a prominent U.S. business publication, the new management elaborated on its revamping of the whole Spanish company, boasting that its efforts had succeeded in rejuvenating the floundering Spanish operation. Naturally, the article found its way back to the Spanish public and greatly angered the Spanish who were associated with the company. In fact, the blunder was so serious that it resulted in a general slowdown of work. (Strikes were then officially banned.)

The Spanish press released an extremely damaging attack, and local authorities made the conduct of the company's business very difficult. The result: the newly acquired subsidiary lost a great deal of its previous business.

Poor Personnel Choices

Just as in any domestic employment position, if a firm places an inappropriate person in an international job, the results can prove disastrous. Several companies have blundered by placing culturally insensitive individuals in sensitive management and sales positions overseas.

A friend of mine reports that he was involved in negotiations with Saudis to sell them material to clean up oil spills. As the deal was about to be closed, a U.S. bank was invited to send some of its people to a closing meeting in Switzerland. The senior banker attending the meeting was well informed of the details of the proposed deal, but it became painfully obvious that at least one of his assistants needed more careful briefing and training when the subject of financing the deal came up. The assistant was asked how he wanted it done and he replied, "It does not matter unless the buyers are Arabs. You can't trust those Arabs."

Interestingly enough, the Saudis were mature enough to realize that one person does not necessarily represent the attitude of the entire bank. When the senior banker immediately apologized, the Saudis simply said they needed time to think things over. They then privately told the senior banker that they would still use his bank and could work with him, but would not under any circumstances work with his anti-Arab assistant. The point was not lost on anyone—including the assistant (who is no longer working for that bank).

In one case, a firm introduced a technical product into a market relatively free of competition. Believing that market entry would pose no problem, the company did not pay enough attention to the personal characteristics of the man it chose as its European sales manager. This was unfortunate. The individual chosen disliked the French and made no effort to ingratiate himself or learn their culture or language. His dislike even spilled over to his abrupt treatment of the sales force. A competitor soon came along and was able to take over much of the market and most of the man's original sales force.

Similarly, an executive from Lucerne, Switzerland, negotiating a business venture with a Japanese firm failed to recognize the importance of personal sentiment to the Japanese and he paid the price. The president of the Japanese company sponsored a party in Tokyo and exclaimed, "I will not do business with a man who does not like us!" The Lucerne executive believed he had concealed his dislike for the Japanese during his stay, but the president of the Japanese company had seen through his mask. The Japanese executive, therefore, refused to proceed with the business deal even though the partnership would undoubtedly have proven mutually profitable.

An employee's attitude, however, is not the only variable of importance. A person may be well intended but simply not be qualified for the job. Several such cases can be cited. A major U.S. appliance manufacturer, for instance, experiencing difficulties in Spain, sent three troubleshooters to investigate. The company overlooked one important fact: the individuals could not speak Spanish. After repeated efforts to communicate failed, the Spaniards eventually lost respect for the three specialists. The problems worsened until a Spanish-speaking manager was sent to help. A similar situation occurred in Germany. A U.S. manager who understood only a little German was sent to Germany to discuss marketing plans with the local subsidiary managers. The local managers, however, spoke little English. Both sides tried to understand each other, but neither nationality did very well. Eventually they parted, thinking that they were in agreement. It was later discovered that during the meeting many important points were overlooked, and the company subsequently lost numerous sales opportunities.

Even though a manager maintains the right attitude and speaks the language, a successful performance is not assured. Raytheon hired Italian-Americans to manage operations in Sicily but found that the strategy was not as effective as hoped. In this case the trouble lay in the origins of the managers. Because their family ties were with the mainland and not Sicilian, these men were not trusted or accepted.

An effective expatriate manager must possess special abilities and traits if he or she is to avoid blundering. Among the most important characteristics are:

- An ability to get along well with people.
- An awareness of cultural differences.
- Open-mindedness.
- Tolerance of foreign cultures.
- Adaptability to new cultures, ideas, and challenges.
- The ability to adjust quickly to new conditions.
- An interest in facts, not blind assumptions.
- Previous business experience.
- Previous experience with foreign cultures.
- The ability to learn foreign languages.

This list is by no means complete. With so many necessary characteristics, it is no wonder that business people sometimes make mistakes.

Labor Relations

Many non-American companies have experienced difficulties adjusting to U.S. labor practices when they acquire U.S. firms. The Japanese have received the most attention concerning this, but Europeans have also run up against their share of troubles. Britain's Grand Met, for example, angered Pillsbury's minority employees when, as the new owner, it fired several black middle managers (including the head of its affirmative action program). In another case, a European firm lost a talented employee when it purchased a company and expected a female executive to start serving coffee at the board meetings.

Because of cultural similarities, a Japanese company doing business in Indonesia consistently hired Bataks, members of an ethnic group with characteristics similar to the Japanese. Other Indonesians, however, resented this hiring practice, viewed it as discriminatory, and forced the company to change its policy.

A U.S. tin mining firm had problems retaining employees in Bolivia even though it paid the employees more than the local competition did. It seems that the problem lay with the method of payment. The U.S. company paid on time every week, but the Bolivians preferred to be paid by the hour. Thus, they could take a few hours off from time to time and not risk the loss of an entire week's wages.

Americans ran into trouble in Iran long before the Iranian revolution. One problem encountered by business people was the widespread belief that foreigners discriminated against Iranians. A U.S. company cemented this belief when it promised local employees that U.S. workers would not be treated preferentially but then provided better health benefits for the U.S. employees.

Verbal promises are taken very seriously in Iran, so the firm's failure to keep its promise was viewed as a major breach of trust and further evidence that foreigners discriminate against Iranians.

Many companies have faced labor troubles in Europe, where governments tend to protect employees and often make layoffs difficult. Some of the most sensationalized cases have occurred in France. Shortly after World War II ended, many U.S. companies rushed into France, hired people, and enjoyed the ensuing business boom. However, the good times didn't last for ever and more than a few firms made the mistake of trying to reduce employment levels. General Motors, Remington Rand, General Electric, and other firms soon found themselves in trouble and were forced to reverse layoff decisions.

Italy has also been the scene of many unpleasant labor disputes with U.S. firms. Raytheon's layoff attempts eventually forced it to close its plant in Sicily at a loss of many millions of dollars.

Another U.S. firm experienced a different kind of problem. The company had a tradition of holding picnics where management and workers mingled with ease in a comfortable environment, so the firm tried to export its company picnic to Spain. To highlight management's "democratic" beliefs, the U.S. executives even dressed as chefs and served the food. However, the picnic failed to help develop the desired rapport between the U.S. managers and the Spanish workers. In fact, it was a very awkward event, as the lower-level staff clung together and did not want to be served by their superiors. When an executive approached the picnic table, everyone stood up. The company quickly learned that Spanish attitudes of class distinction and social groups make casual mixing and socializing of workers with executives very difficult.

The United Kingdom has been the home for some of the best-known labor problems of U.S. companies. Ford

Motor Company, for example, ran into hard times in England because the British managers and laborers felt that the U.S. managers there were treated better and were given more power. Many employees openly resented this apparent favoritism. Several key British executives even quit. The company lowered the number of Americans there and this reduced the problem, but decisions from headquarters were still resented. At one point, British newspapers ran such headlines as "Local Ford plants can't even build a bathroom without permission from Detroit." Actually, this was not far from the truth at the time. Now, much more power is delegated to the local managers (who are more likely now to be British) and Ford's labor relations are much better.

The Roberts Arundel textile machinery plant in Stockport, England had to close down after managers tried to impose U.S. labor practices. Mr. Arundel later admitted that it was a mistake to try to change worker habits, but they had thought that production line work would go better if those famous tea breaks were dropped. Employees thought otherwise! It is usually easier to change management practices than radically alter local work habits.

SUMMARY

Obviously, management practices that work domestically do not necessarily work overseas. Different cultures require that companies take different approaches. Managers need to understand local business procedures, governmental expectations, and labor practices. A minor misunderstanding can easily lead to a major blunder and the wrong person on the job can lead to disaster.

CHAPTER 7

Strategic Management

- Entry Mode
- Supply Problems
- Complex Problems
- Additional Mistakes
- Summary

CHAPTER 7

Strategic Management

Companies have committed a wide variety of strategic mistakes over the years. Many have been related to their choice of how to enter the foreign market. Supply decisions, though, have also caused a surprising number of problems. Some of the strategic errors have involved fairly complex issues. Naturally, all of these blunders were regretted.

Entry Mode

A company which is "going international" has a variety of entry methods available to it. Acquiring an existing firm, starting up a new operation, forming a joint venture with a local company, and signing licensing agreements are some of the most popular modes of entry. Each method offers advantages and disadvantages.

It might seem that the creation of a joint venture, for example, would eliminate all of the problems encountered by a company "going overseas." With the combined expertise and efforts of both local and foreign firms, major problems or possible blunders would surely be eliminated. However, although certain types of errors are definitely less likely, a multitude of other problems can arise and pose serious threats to the venture's success.

More than a few firms have experienced unexpected problems with joint ventures. One U.S. firm that entered into a joint venture with some South American capitalists did not fully comprehend its initial errors until some five years later. At the time of the company's commitment, its South American partners were temporarily in favor with those in the local government. However, the joint venture began to gradually experience various forms of host government harassment and, consequently, profits slowly declined. The U.S. partner lost investment money, effort, and time. What had happened? They had failed to analyze the situation thoroughly. Early analyses should have revealed both the existence of a volatile political scene and the high degree of political involvement in local business practices.

Dow Chemical Company's joint venture in Korea failed for many reasons, but one important cause was poor communication. Misunderstandings were everywhere and communication seemed to get nowhere. The situation became so bad that Dow Chemical decided to go public with complaints about its partner. This, of course, infuriated the Koreans. Asians tend to keep problems very private, so Dow's strategy of applying public pressure backfired. The Koreans, in fact, felt that they had no choice but to withdraw from the joint venture, as anything else would be viewed as a further loss of face.

A company should create a joint venture only after giving the idea careful consideration. Although another firm may be "willing and waiting" to become a partner, its eagerness does not necessarily assure success. One U.S. manager found this to be especially true. During an inspection of his company's European operations, he met with a number of Belgian pump manufacturing executives. Because one particular company exhibited a great deal of interest in forming a partnership, a joint enterprise was quickly formed. A Belgian was established as the president of the new company, and the U.S. firm's manager in Belgium became the vice-president for manufacturing and engineering. However, friction between these two men and company losses precipitated a crisis. The partnership was dissolved, and the U.S. company bought up all of the Belgian shares at book value. The result: it was many years before the operation became profitable. Undoubtedly, the U.S. firm's unfortunate choice of a partner hindered this venture's success. Partners must be selected with caution, and employee personalities should be considered.

A bakery products firm contracted to sell its entire line of baked goods through a sole distributor in a developing country. The distributor had really only been interested in carrying a few items and found the tie-in arrangement disagreeable. Therefore, relations between the manufacturer and distributor quickly degenerated to the point where little communication existed between them. A serious decline in sales subsequently occurred. Unfortunately, this information did not reach the manufacturer very quickly and large quantities of baked goods spoiled.

Although blunders are often caused by a company's failure to thoroughly investigate potential partners, sometimes a firm's failure to take advantage of a possible joint venture or licensing agreement also results in a suboptimal situation. For instance, parts "specifically for use in" equipment manufactured by the Caterpillar Tractor Company began surfacing for sale in various markets. These products had neither been approved nor manufactured by the Caterpillar Company. The firm, however, was unable to establish any legal claims. If the company had initially sought out a local partner, the demand for these similar parts most assuredly would have benefited Caterpillar. As it turned out, the local manufacturers saw no reason to avoid competing with the totally foreign-owned Caterpillar Tractor Company.

Licensing decisions are as difficult to analyze as those decisions involving the creation of a joint venture. Failure to make the correct decision at the right time can result in the loss of substantial long-range business prospects and potential profits. In one case, a U.S. manufacturer not only licensed the manufacture and sale of its products to an English firm but also granted the firm the exclusive right to sublicense the U.S. expertise to other countries. At the time the decision was made, the company was not interested in expanding overseas. The firm believed that it was best to simply collect the royalties and thus eliminate its need to provide additional investment money. Within a few years, worldwide markets for the firm's products developed. Naturally, the company greatly regretted its earlier decision to permit exclusive licensing.

A similar case involved a U.S. pharmaceutical firm which licensed its manufacturing techniques to an Asian company. The Asian company, heavily promoting the products, enjoyed great success. As a result of the licensing terms, however, the Asian company reaped almost all of the tremendous profits. Having never realized the product's potential, the U.S. company had permitted the licensing. If the U.S. firm had committed to a more direct form of involvement, such as equity participation, it could have earned greater profits. In this instance, the company's failure to carefully study the market and product opportunities eventually resulted in a lost opportunity.

Sometimes the licensee, although pleased to have been granted the license, is not as enthusiastic about the product as the licensor. One U.S. firm discovered this when it granted an exclusive license to a Japanese company. The Japanese company was given the right to manufacture and sell one of the U.S. firm's specialty products for a period of 20 years. Market studies had indicated that the product, which had been extremely successful in the United States, was destined to replace some of the more conventional materials currently in use in Japan. The U.S. firm had carefully studied its potential licensees and had chosen the Japanese company because of its strength of distribution, size, and record of profit performance. However, the Japanese firm, continuing to push the more conventional materials, failed to promote the new product actively. Since the contract included no agreement concerning minimum royalties, the U.S. company earned no income for the first 10 years. Having failed to recognize the Japanese company's marketing initiatives and lack of interest, the U.S. firm was forced to accept the fact that it could not enter the market itself until the expiration of the 20-year license.

The natural tendency for any company is to "get in while the going is good." One U.S. firm particularly eager to begin operations in India quickly negotiated terms and completed arrangements with its local partners. Certain required documents, however, such as the industrial license, foreign collaboration agreements, capital issues permit, import licenses for machinery and equipment, etc., were slow in being issued. Trying to expedite governmental approval of these items, the U.S. firm agreed to accept a lower royalty fee than originally stipulated. Despite all of this extra effort, the project was not greatly expedited, and the lower royalty fee reduced the firm's profit by approximately half of a million dollars over the life of the agreement.

Warner-Lambert ran into major problems trying to sell "Trident," "Chiclets," and other brands of chewing gum to the Japanese. Because its local wholesalers were not promoting the products to the extent Warner-Lambert desired, the firm decided to change its strategy. The company tried to bypass its wholesalers but quickly realized its mistake. Not only did this move upset the wholesalers; it also created suspicions among the retailers who often consider companies unreliable if they switch business tactics. To recover, the company asked its sales force to collect the retail sales orders for the wholesalers.

Heinz also experienced difficulties with the Japanese market. Attempting to enter the market quickly, Heinz gained a minority interest in a company called Nichiro Fisheries. Not only did the fishery name imply that all the products were fish-oriented, but the partnership simply was not appropriate. Nichiro Fisheries did not hold enough capital nor did it maintain the broad distribution channels necessary to market Heinz's products adequately.

Failing to consider the values or reliability of a potential partner can also prove disastrous. In some countries, it is normal for a company to take whatever it can from its partner. When both parties expect this, reasonable safeguards can be established. When one company is not aware of this practice, though, blunders can certainly result. For example, a U.S. chemical manufacturer agreed to a partnership after being visited by some overseas managers. The strategy developed involved the export of raw materials by the U.S. firm and the manufacture of products by the foreign company. All of the details were carefully stipulated in the contract, but within six months of the first large shipment of raw materials, the partnership broke up. What had gone wrong? Credit terms had not been met, earnings were disputed, and payments had not been sent. The well-known and "respected" local partner had gained part of his visibility through his ability to delay or avoid paying his obligations—a common local practice. The U.S. company should have been aware of this local custom. It then would have known to require payment in advance (the locally accepted practice) or could have established some other financially safe arrangement. To the local courts, the U.S. firm appeared foolish and deserved the loss—after all, the company had failed to follow sound, normal, business practices.

Supply Problems

Most companies try to save money by purchasing supplies in large quantities. There are, however, logical limits governing this strategy. One example of excessive purchasing occurred in Chile. The Chilean government used to have high tariffs on automobile imports. Over time, this policy created a large pent-up demand for cars. In the late 1970s the government began to radically reduce tariffs and, consequently, demand quickly out-stripped supply. By 1981 these tariffs had dropped so low that large numbers of Chileans could afford new autos. Because dealers were unable to fill the vast number of orders, a five-month waiting period for most automobile models was not unusual. Believing that this demand might be unlimited, dealers ordered up to ten times their normal number of cars for 1982 even though the economy began experiencing a recession and the new models were higher-priced. A flooded market resulted. Most of the demand for autos had already been satisfied, and few of the fairly new cars needed to be replaced. Economic uncertainty and higher prices also kept customers away. The result was that inventories grew so high that dealers had no room to store the cars. Many loads (more than a year's supply) were left on board ships lying offshore, incurring high storage costs. The lesson: optimistic, straight-line projections of sales figures are obviously dangerous. Temporary causes of demand should be analyzed and estimates made to determine the amount of pent-up demand still remaining.

Nigeria, though, probably experienced the largest purchasing blunder. Due to increased oil revenues that resulted from the sharp rise of oil prices in the mid-1970s, Nigeria began to initiate major modernization programs. An economically minded bureaucrat decided to purchase, mostly from other countries, the total amount of cement needed to construct all of the new buildings being planned. Soon the cement began to arrive by the shipload. The dockworkers were unable to unload the cement as fast as it arrived, so the ships were forced to await their turn for unloading. Within weeks, there were so many shiploads of unloaded cement that someone computed the length of time required to unload all of the ships. Even with an expanded dock in Lagos, it was calculated that the 20 million tons of cement could not be fully unloaded for 40 years! Much of the cement had to be dumped overboard. The cost to hold the ships until unloading was greater than the cost of reordering the cement.

EverReady, of England, encountered supply problems of a different nature. Hoping to introduce its product to the Nigerians, the company chose a strategy that stressed broad market penetration. The EverReady name and battery were heavily promoted, and a large production run was shipped to Lagos. No problems occurred during the unloading, but the firm probably wished that some had. Apparently a defective chemical had been used during the production of the batteries, and those shipped to Lagos were worthless. Unfortunately, someone had forgotten to test them prior to shipment. Although the first batteries appearing on the heavily promoted Nigerian market sold quickly, word soon spread that the product was not dependable. Since no backup supply of good batteries was available, the promotional effort was wasted, and the firm developed a reputation in Nigeria as being an unreliable company which produced poor goods. Later, when normal batteries reached the Nigerian market, consumers avoided them. It took years for EverReady to overcome its initial reputation there.

Large department stores often purchase stock from many sources, including foreign countries. It is especially important for the buyers of these goods to be familiar with local foreign customs. They should also be fluent in the required language or have translation assistance. One overconfident buyer created quite a problem for her Italian firm. Believing that she knew English fairly well, she was sent to Britain to purchase clothing. When she found some appropriate sweaters at Bourne & Hollingsworth, she attempted to request "four to five thousand pounds' worth." It became quite obvious, however, that there had been a "misunderstanding" when she returned to Italy and the delivery trucks began arriving. They were carrying the "forty-five" thousand pounds' worth (approximately U.S.$90,000) that she had actually ordered!

Often a company is initially successful overseas but later experiences major difficulties. This occurred to one company that was located in Africa. The firm began purchasing huge supplies of old, used inner tubes discarded by the U.S. Army during World War II. These inexpensive discards were easily cut to form rubber bands, and soon the company had captured the entire local rubber band market. After making over $1 million on the venture, the owners felt extremely clever and successful until someone pointed out that the supply of old inner tubes had dried up. The war was over, the army had left, and the newer tires of the few vehicles still in use were tubeless. Awash with money and confidence, the managers decided to "go big league" and buy modern equipment. The machinery and supplies, of course, were expensive and quite difficult to maintain. The company, unskilled in the new process, and failing to realize how different the new system would be, was unable to produce rubber bands at affordable prices. The strategy failed, and all of the former profits were lost.

Supply difficulties have hindered a number of companies. As was mentioned in the second chapter, one U.S. pineapple firm was unable to transport its fruit down the river to its processing plant because it had failed to analyze the typical river conditions. Similarly, the Soviet Union built a large, expensive steel mill for India only to discover that the mill had been located in an area without adequate transportation facilities. The steel mill, intended as a showplace for Soviet propaganda purposes, became an embarrassment instead.

Another firm developed problems when it tried to buy steel plates from Japanese manufacturers. At the root of this blunder was the company's failure to understand the Japanese tendency to answer "yes." By inviting all of the Japanese plate producers to bid, the company felt that it would attain the lowest price. The low bidder offered to sell at such an appealing price that the firm decided to order all of the needed galvanized steel plates from that particular Japanese company. The Japanese firm was first contacted, however, to assure product availability, since the quantity required was so large. "Yes" the company responded; it would fulfill the large order. The U.S. corporation confidently awaited the shipment. Eventually a small, partial shipment arrived containing plates that had obviously been hand dipped. Since, during the normal production process, machines do all of the dipping, the U.S. firm became suspicious. Upon visiting the Japanese plant, its suspicions were confirmed. The plant was quite small and simply could not supply the necessary quantities. Although the Japanese managers knew this would be the case, they did not want to lose face by admitting that their company was so small. They had simply hoped that all would work out.

Complex Problems

Although some of the strategic errors committed by multinational corporations are fairly easy to understand, others are complex and involve several components. Simmons, Ford, Raytheon, and General Electric have all experienced complex problems within their foreign operations.

The Simmons Company, a marketer of quality beds, might never have taken the plunge to expand to Japan if it had known the magnitude of the problems it would encounter. With numerous successful overseas ventures under its belt and confident of its product, the Simmons Company set out in the early 1960s to manufacture mattresses in Japan. Four years later, the company was still experiencing substantial losses in Japan. Several complex problems plagued its operation. Although aware of many of the difficulties surrounding the Japanese market, the company had underestimated the degree of complexity present in the Japanese environment.

Simmons had realized that it would face several obstacles. Not only did most Japanese still sleep on futons (a type of floor mat), but the company also recognized that the complex and unusual Japanese distribution system could be quite confusing. The fact that an oligopolistic group of local manufacturers vied for control of the limited market only complicated matters further.

However, because the firm strongly believed in its product and know-how, Simmons Tokyo (later, Simmons Japan) was organized in October 1964. Entry into the market had been timed to coincide with the Tokyo

Olympic Games when the demand for beds would sharply rise over a short period of time. Early production progressed smoothly, but problems developed later.

Among the difficulties the company encountered was its choice of a sales force. Because of the existence of social class differences and subtle language styles, the salespeople were most effective if they and the client were of the same class. Therefore, the initial eight-man sales force had to be rigorously screened. Even after an appropriate personnel choice, a problem ensued. None of the salesmen had ever slept on a bed! How could they be expected to sincerely endorse Simmons's product?

Simmons also learned that it had priced its beds by as much as $60 above domestic prices. Even the distribution system proved baffling—everyday conduct and favors were often intertwined. A customer might engage in business with a supplier to whom he owed a favor regardless of the price difference, and this behavior produced a tangled distribution network with complex relationships. Since no Japanese wished to lose face, Simmons also discovered that trying to operate outside of this established system was quite difficult.

And finally, Simmons made an unfortunate decision regarding advertising media. The company chose print media and concentrated its distribution in the Tokyo area instead of using television, the most effective and penetrating advertising medium in Japan.

Another U.S. firm encountered other types of problems in its efforts to "go international." A foreign firm interested in creating a joint venture in Asia approached an electronics firm. Because the product potential appeared so high, the company wished to establish the venture fully before any competition could be enticed into the market. So an agreement was quickly arranged. In its haste, however, the U.S. firm failed to investigate completely such important marketing factors as competitive environment, market maturity, distribution requirements, marketing costs, penetration strategy, promotional programs, etc. Also, the U.S. company did not carefully evaluate its partner's experience, general know-how, and operational procedures. As a result, problems that should have been considered and resolved during the initial planning stages of the venture were still cropping up years later.

Ford Motor Company has established a very successful record in international business. In fact, it has been the most successful U.S. automotive company to engage in business outside of North America. Even Ford, however, has encountered its share of troubles. In 1973, for instance, after experiencing great success in the Philippines with the Fiera, Ford introduced the vehicle in Thailand. It sold poorly, however. Ford had overestimated its reputation and had incorrectly assumed that Thai consumers would prefer a Ford to other cars. The company had also assumed that the Fiera's low price would attract customers, but it was not prepared to offer the credit terms extended by its competitors. Furthermore, the Fiera frequently experienced breakdowns because vehicles in Thailand were usually loaded two or three times beyond normally designed capacities. By the time a sturdier model was introduced, the Fiera had already earned a reputation for being unreliable.

When Raytheon's local partner withdrew from its Sicilian joint venture due to declining profits, Raytheon was unable to find a replacement partner for its television tube-producing plant. The plant needed modernization, but the needed modifications required substantial capital investment. Thus, Raytheon tried to continue selling out-of-date tubes. Not only were the tubes outdated, but the market was saturated. The company failed to develop any export markets even though sales dropped significantly in Italy. Losses continued to mount, so the firm fired one-quarter of its employees. The dismissal of Sicilian employees without prior governmental approval and without major payments to those involved, however, was an extremely unacceptable business practice. The result: the local governmental officials took control of the plant, and Raytheon lost over $25 million.

In a different part of Europe, another large U.S. corporation came very close to committing a similar error. To realize substantial cost savings, the company planned a massive cost reduction program that involved the layoff of a significant number of employees. It was fortunate for the company that prior to the initiation of the program it learned that layoffs based on these grounds were highly unacceptable in the host country. Since much of the firm's business was with agencies of the host government, this action surely would have evoked great unhappiness and the government agencies would have been pressured to place their orders with other suppliers. Sales undoubtedly would have dropped, but even more damaging and far-reaching would have been the company's loss of reputation. Indeed the blunder was avoided, but the company had needlessly allocated time and money to develop a plan that never could have worked. Much waste could have been eliminated had the corporation been aware of this local business practice.

General Electric also experienced overseas troubles. The company was initially so optimistic and enthusiastic about some of its foreign ventures that its original projections and timetables were unrealistic and consequently led to disappointment. Because of these early letdowns, management tended to be wary of complete ownership or majority interest in its overseas operations. And in some South American projects the company tried too long to maintain the distribution channels it had developed over the years. By doing so, it became particularly vulnerable to the rise of innovative competition during a period of rapidly changing environments and thus failed to aggressively seek out and adopt new methods of distribution.

Additional Mistakes

Embarrassing and expensive slip-ups can result when firms cut back. During strategic moves, such as downsizing, some of the employees who remain may not have received proper training in order to handle international transactions appropriately. Such was the case for the Carlson Travel Network when one client, a manufacturing executive, was traveling from Japan to Taiwan. Upon arrival in Taiwan the executive arrived without the proper visa. Through the fault of the employee at the travel network, the executive spent 18 hours on a return trip to his home office, unable to finish his business trip. The expense to the network was a second ticket, upgraded to first class, and incidental expenses of the first trip.

Sometimes a company finds that its golden touch is not golden everywhere. The Tengelmann group of West Germany discovered this when it bought a U.S. supermarket chain, the A&P. The firm's normal strategy of offering a limited line of low-cost, store brand groceries worked well for Tengelmann in Europe. However, its attempts to use this same strategy in the United States failed and resulted in a $75 million loss over a two-year period. As the chairman, James Wood, reported, "The mistake we foreigners often make is to judge the U.S. on the basis of what we know about Europe. Americans want a fuller range of products from a supermarket than people on the other side of the water."[1]

Foreign firms often get tripped up in the United States because they fail to develop clear strategies unique to their U.S. operations. Extensions of home strategies often are inappropriate, but foreign-owned firms seem determined to learn this the hard way. The purchase of the A.B. Dick Company by General Electric of Britain is a case in point. Because the British firm did well in the United Kingdom advertising and selling its "modern" office products, it promoted this theme when marketing A.B. Dick products in the United States. The problem? Eighty percent of the A.B. Dick products were not modern, and so the company's strategy was ineffective.

Europeans, of course, are not the only ones who sometimes assume that what works at home will also work abroad. A highly successful U.S. supermarket chain experienced difficulties in its overseas venture. The U.S. company and a renowned Japanese company, Sumitomo Shoji Kaisha, formed a supermarket joint venture in Japan. Small Japanese retailers, however, strongly objected to the bond created by these two giants, so Sumitomo Shoji helped set up a dummy company and permitted the U.S. firm to manage it. The U.S. company employed the techniques proven successful in U.S. supermarket management but could not produce profitable financial statements in Japan. After studying the Japanese distribution system, the Japanese traditional ways of doing business, and the characteristics of the Japanese customers, the U.S. management decided that it was necessary to convert the operations to a "Japanese mode." The Japanese customers found the new system acceptable, and the venture began to thrive.

Parker Pen decided to streamline its product line and "globalize" its operations. Parker reduced its global product line from 500 styles in about 150 countries to 100 pen styles and decided to use a single international campaign. The concept sounded fine and certainly permitted real production and marketing savings, but it created serious morale problems for Parker's managers. Overseas managers resented the U.S. mandated plan. Profits sank, management rebelled, and the strategy was eventually discontinued. Parker Pen now lets local managers determine promotional plans.

In another case, a U.S. consumer products firm developed a plan to create a world structure of subsidiaries through the acquisition of similar companies located in both developed and developing countries. Through these subsidiaries, it hoped to form a worldwide market for its products. Therefore, small and medium-sized companies in Europe, Latin America, and Japan were purchased within a three-year period. Special efforts were made to add the U.S. products to the existing lines of the acquired companies, since the consumer goods available through these foreign companies were different from those in the parent's line.

However, the U.S. company ran into several problems using this strategy. Not only had it failed to consider the tastes of its potential customers, in most cases the U.S. products did not even meet foreign requirements. Furthermore, the marketing, advertising, and promotional techniques that had produced such a long record of company success in the United States were not appropriate for the foreign environments. Because of the lack of supermarkets and retail chain outlets, lower standards of living, limited television advertising exposure, and lower levels of literacy, the U.S. techniques proved ineffective in these new markets.

Many cases can be cited to illustrate the importance of conducting a thorough preliminary market study. Consider, for example, the U.S. company that discovered its failure to understand its Japanese partner's distribution network greatly hindered the venture's success. Hoping to achieve optimum market penetration for its product, that was relatively new to the Japanese, the U.S. firm selected the best distribution networks of its Japanese partner and set up a single-level system of wholesalers. Even though the product sold well through the selected distribution channels, market penetration fell short of expectation because the product did not receive the needed national coverage. The original decision to use the partner's best distribution networks appeared wise, but the firm failed to fully realize how numerous and diffuse the Japanese retail outlet networks can be and overestimated the effectiveness of its planned network.

Distribution problems do not only occur within the Japanese system. Having received encouraging results from a preliminary market study, a major U.S. manufacturer of mixed feed for poultry decided to establish a market in Spain. Although local business people advised the firm against forming a subsidiary that was wholly owned, the company went ahead with its plans. A factory was built, technical staff was brought in, and operations were set up. However, once production began, the firm discovered that it could not sell its products. Why? The Spanish poultry growers and feed producers comprised a closely knit group, and newcomers were not welcome. To overcome this obstacle, the firm bought a series of chicken farms. To its dismay, the company discovered that no one would buy its chickens either! Had the company heeded the local advice and understood the local business practices, these difficulties could have been avoided.

Many other companies have suffered from similar pitfalls. For instance, one U.S. cosmetics manufacturer experienced difficulties when it tried to sell its products in France solely through a chain store. By utilizing this method, the firm felt it could achieve maximum market exposure while still holding down marketing and distribution costs. In some countries, this system might have worked. In France, however, "perfumers" (small local retailers specializing in cosmetics) are traditionally considered the opinion makers, and most manufacturers give exclusive franchise to two or three local perfumers. Word-of-mouth promotion is vital, and the public relies heavily on the opinions of these perfumers. When it bypassed them, the U.S. company angered the perfumers to the point that they discredited the U.S. product and damaged the manufacturer's reputation in France.

A clear, consistent strategy is required if a company is to succeed in the international marketplace. Asuag A6, a Swiss watchmaker, realized this too late. The firm needed to acquire technology and decided to do so by purchasing a dozen different U.S. firms. Although some of the companies proved useful to the watchmaker, they did not seem to fit together well. Many were not even compatible with others in the acquisition package. Trying to work them together only made matters worse. All 12 were eventually sold—at a loss of over $25 million.

Fujitec, a Japanese elevator manufacturer, came to the United States with high aspirations—too high, as it turned out. Rather than concentrate on one geographical area, the firm simultaneously sought out large projects all over the country. However, it apparently failed to recognize the regional preferences of U.S. consumers and tried to approach the market as if none existed. As a consequence, the company did not consider important cultural subtleties and lost money. Japan may be a fairly homogeneous market, but the U.S. market is not. Few companies have the ability to enter all regions at the same time. Most find that they need business experience in one or two regions of the United States before they can attempt a national campaign.

Companies have experienced many difficulties as a result of poor strategy decisions. As an illustration, consider the aerospace division of Ling-Temco-Vought (LTV), which tried to create a mechanical substitute for the water buffalo. Because the company's research and development facilities were located in the United States, the firm developed the machine there. Unfortunately this was not a wise decision. The machines produced by the company were eventually exposed to the unique Asian weather conditions and experienced numerous problems.

An unfortunate decision made by Gillette nearly cost the company the razor blade market. The firm had developed a superior stainless steel blade, but because the new blade was so outstanding and would require fewer replacements, the company preferred not to market it. So Gillette sold the technology to a British garden tool manufacturer, Wilkinson. Because Gillette had assumed that Wilkinson would only use the new technology in the production of its garden tools, it failed to restrict Wilkinson from competing in the razor blade market. However, Wilkinson Sword blades were promptly introduced and sold as fast as they could be produced. Gillette's superior marketing skills and experience in the razor blade market enabled it to eventually recover, but the challenge was unwelcome and expensive.

SUMMARY

False assumptions frequently cause expensive blunders. One of the most common assumptions is that conditions that exist at home also exist abroad. Another frequently assumed idea is that what works well at home will also work well overseas. It should be abundantly clear that these are two of the most dangerous assumptions that can be made by managers. Few things are the same everywhere, and almost no strategy works well everywhere.

Strategic blunders are generally not as entertaining to read about as some of the other international business mistakes, but they are usually more critical to the firm and thus more important to avoid. Although some mistakes can be quickly corrected, logistical problems can be very difficult to overcome. A few strategic blunders have even resulted in millions of lost dollars. There are no simple short cuts to avoid strategic errors. The development of a strategy requires care and attention to detail.

Other Areas of International Business

- Legal
- Finance
- Market Research
- Summary

CHAPTER 8

Other Areas of International Business

The previous chapters have contained numerous examples of blunders made in the areas of production, translation, name choices, marketing, management, and strategy. These types of blunders are frequently committed and often quite visible. Once made, these mistakes can be rather difficult to conceal. Blunders occurring in the other areas of business, such as law, finance, and market research, are either less frequently committed or easier to hide. They certainly are not reported as often, but they can be just as costly or critical to the success of the business venture.

Legal

The legal details involved in any transaction certainly can seem confusing and boring. However, a lack of awareness or understanding of these technicalities can prove to be disastrous, as illustrated in the plight of a U.S. person transacting business in Saudi Arabia. A Californian is reported to have found himself trapped in Saudi Arabia as a result of a dispute he was having with his Saudi partner. The Saudi, an associate in a janitorial supplies venture, had sponsored his Californian partner's entry into Saudi Arabia, but refused to sponsor the man's departure unless he was paid the $100,000 he claimed was due him. Under Saudi law, a foreigner can not leave the country without the endorsement of the person who sponsored his entry! The American settled by paying $55,000. "It was the only way I could get out," he said. The problem might have been avoided if he had insisted in advance on a written agreement with the Saudi.

A U.S. firm discovered the value of using clear and concise contractual language when one of its West African contract clauses cost the company about $100,000. The troublesome clause read, "The monies paid by the Ministry to the Consultant shall constitute full payment to the Consultant including all local income taxes on the Consultant." The firm understood this to mean that payments were tax-free. The government ruled otherwise. And since another clause in the contract said that disagreements were to be settled by the local government, the firm lost.

One large firm went to China with a 50-plus page legal document to license pollution control technology. The Chinese laughed at them, tossed it out, and the proposed deal would have fallen through, but because good personal relations had been established, they allowed the firm to start over. A 10-page document was then developed and accepted.

A big firm in China wanted a contract and agreed to two versions: one in English and the other in Chinese. "Both versions shall have equal force." This later led to many problems and costly debates.

A Columbus, Ohio company committed a "minor" error in filling out a form in Brazil. Unfortunately, this mistake resulted in the firm being unable to withdraw $200,000 in profits it eventually earned there. What was the "minor" error? Someone had failed to place a check in a box on the document that would have allowed the company to withdraw profits at a reasonable rate.

AT&T experienced troubles in Thailand in 1989 trying to obtain a major phone equipment contract. After a great deal of effort, AT&T submitted a proposal but it was promptly rejected. Apparently, Thailand had specified that a 10-year warranty was required, but the AT&T lawyers working out of the United States proposed a five-year warranty. The company's employees and contacts in Thailand understood the requirement, but the contract had been drawn up by lawyers thousands of miles away. In fact, AT&T has had such relatively little on-the-scene overseas experience that as late as 1989, . when an emergency meeting was called in Italy, several of its U.S.-based "international" managers had to reveal that they did not even own a passport.

Most countries have now established regulations dealing with advertising. As many companies can avow, failure to follow these guidelines almost always results in a legal dispute. Singapore's airline can attest to this. The company placed advertisements in local Norwegian magazines featuring a photo of a girl's face on a pillow. The message essentially said "Bring me a pillow and brandy for a tired father." The Norwegians were upset with the ad, and eventually the promotion was ruled misleading and sexually discriminating.

Similarly, the use of a commercial featuring a bikini-clad woman created difficulties for Goodyear. The advertisement was apparently shown in several countries where the skimpy attire was not locally permitted. The company was forced to alter the commercial and so replaced the young beauty with fully dressed people having a good time. The message, "Get where the fun is," remained unchanged, but the "new" commercial was considered more acceptable and effective.

Goodyear Tire also experienced legal problems with an advertisement it tried to export to Germany. The ad, successfully used in the United States, highlighted the strength of Goodyear's tire cord by showing that it could break a steel chain. Goodyear discovered, however, that in Germany it was illegal to imply that another product was inferior. Because Goodyear's promotion was interpreted to be disparaging to the German steel chain manufacturers, the government halted the promotional campaign.

Toyota learned that they need to be aware of the claims they make with an ad, especially when adapting to the Chinese culture. The Chinese are well known for their high standards for truth in advertising. This applies to foreign companies who enter the Chinese market. The case of Toyota's advertising campaign is based on an old Chinese proverb that read, "When you get to the foot of the mountain, a road will appear." The Toyota ad read, "Wherever there is a road, there is a Toyota." It was one year after all the slogans appeared on billboards, on television, and in newspapers when the Chinese authorities claimed that Toyota was guilty of false advertising. The reasons given by the Chinese officials included that "China has roads but there are not necessarily Toyotas on them. The roads in other countries do not necessarily have them either." As a result, Toyota learned the difference between standards in a strict socialist advertising society verses a more lax capitalistic society.

Claridge cigarettes advertised its product in Australia using a campaign that featured Robin Hood and Friar Tuck. Australians, believing that their children might find the ad appealing, felt that the orientation was inappropriate and they forced Claridge to alter its advertisements.

Ford experienced a similar problem with one of its ads distributed in Norway. The advertisement featured children talking to a car salesman, with the caption "Is it true that there is a waiting period for Fords?" Local groups complained that it was improper to use the children in the promotion because they were not directly connected to the product. While such use could easily be considered harmless and enjoyable by many, a firm must consider potential legal expenses should it find itself defending its ads.

A novel twist occurred in France, where Philip Morris and the R.J. Reynolds Tobacco Company were enjoying much financial success. The companies, in fact, were so successful that a local company, SEITA, tried to sell its cigarettes as if they, too, were foreign imports. Their packages bore the name "News" and were printed totally in English. Not even the well-known French name of the parent company was listed. French law, however, prohibited this omission, and so, in this case, it was the local company that experienced the legal difficulties in its effort to thwart foreign competition.

The complexities of foreign investment laws have also been frequent sources of problems. The 3M Company, for example, submitted an application to the Japanese government to establish a joint venture with 15 firms of the Sumitomo industrial group. The company's failure to consider all of the applicable Japanese investment laws delayed the governmental approval required. By the time the approval was obtained—four years later—domestic manufacturers such as Sony and Tokyo Denki Kagaka had succeeded in streamlining the production of magnetic tape products and, unfortunately, Sumitomo-3M's share of the market was held to a very small percentage of the total Japanese market.

False assumptions regarding the level of host government support have led to many problems. Massey-Ferguson, for example, believed it had won Turkish support to establish a tractor-producing plant. The company heavily relied on that support to help with sales. Unfortunately, the support never materialized and the venture eventually died.

Sometimes companies win governmental support when perhaps they should not. It is, for example, possible at times to gain legal approval to do (or not do) things which should not (or should) be done. This legal support offers a business protection but it can prove to be temporary or controversial. Several firms have found all too suddenly that, as times change, the definition of what is acceptable can change.

Consider a company in Spain that obtained permission from the Spanish government to use badly outdated technology which polluted the atmosphere. A sudden change in weather created a dangerous health situation, however. Several people died, the local population rioted, the government withdrew its approval, and the company paid the price for hiding behind the legal protection of the government.

Several U.S. firms have encountered legal problems either at home or abroad because they were affiliated in some way with overseas business operations which "traded with the enemy." U.S. law sometimes forbids U.S. firms to sell certain products to certain countries. Special problems can arise when overseas joint ventures or even licensed firms start trading with these outlawed countries. If the U.S. parent or partner company does not restrict business activity, the U.S. government takes legal action. But, if the U.S. parent or partner discontinues the business overseas, the host government may take legal action of its own. Just because the U.S. government restricts business activities in a country does not mean that all countries curtail business operations there. This can be an awkward, Catch 22-type situation—one that is best avoided by anticipating the potential problem and clarifying everything before formalizing any joint venture or signing any agreement.

For example, Fruehauf, a U.S. truck manufacturer, sold truck bodies to a French firm through its French subsidiary. The French firm then finished the trucks and sold them to the People's Republic of China. The U.S. government took action against Fruehauf for selling trucks to China (an outlawed destination at the time). Consequently, this U.S. behavior caused the French government to seize control of Fruehauf's French subsidiary. France believed that Fruehauf had to honor its contracts—even if that meant selling parts which eventually ended up in China (an acceptable destination to the French). Not only did Fruehauf lose money, but the company became the unwanted center of a highly charged public debate in France concerning the role of the United States and its firms in France. At that point, it was clearly a no-win situation that took years to overcome.

It is absolutely critical to remember that what is legal in one country may not be legal in another. This important lesson applies to many aspects of business, including patent protection of industrial property rights. Many firms have falsely assumed that more protection existed in a foreign country than proved to be the case. If companies are not careful, highly valued trade secrets can be lost, with no legal recourse.

Companies may experience troubles by being unaware of a country's regulations and preferences concerning products and packages. The wording on a package or label may create difficulties. Countries expect foreign marketers to adhere to rules, and their failure to do so may prove costly. Coca-Cola, for instance, aroused the anger of the Italians when it printed the mandatory list of ingredients on its bottle cap. Local courts ruled that the cap was easily tossed away and, therefore, did not serve as an acceptable location for this list. Coca-Cola, of course, quickly modified its package and listed the ingredients on the bottles themselves, but the incident had its costs.

Many companies have encountered legal problems trying to sell various diet foods because, in several countries, a product name containing the word "diet" can be sold only in pharmacies. Thus, these lighter-in-calories products can now be found on store shelves in some countries with "Lite" used in their names.

In Australia, the manufacturer of "Aim" toothpaste was taken to court by one of its competitors because of an Australian law that prohibits the sale of competitive products in similar packages. A very strict interpretation and enforcement of this law forced Unilever to change its Aim package even though it had spent $5 million on Aim's promotion. The error was costly, but it was correctable with the appropriate alterations.[1]

Finance

Small overseas firms are sometimes so impressed with the size and growth of U.S. markets that they forget about the possible risk of a U.S. economic downturn. The U.S. economy may be comparatively wealthy to many people, but it still experiences recessions and these need to be taken into consideration by the investing firms. Many foreign-owned firms in the United States have reportedly sunk because they failed to plan for worst case scenarios.

Since most foreign investors in the United States do not have their stock listed on U.S. markets, they seldom make an acquisition through stock swaps. This means that they are usually forced to borrow money. If the timing is poor or if they do not prepare for market downturns, they can be squeezed unexpectedly. For example, Agache-Willot (French) purchased Korvettes but was not prepared to invest another $28 million when a subsequent recession was experienced. By the time the firm finally agreed to infuse the additional needed capital, it was really too late. Korvettes went bankrupt a year later.

U.S. firms have also fallen into the temptation of having a very high debt to equity ratio. This highly leveraged position works well when times are good, but it is risky and can lead to disasters in bad times. The USM subsidiary in Portugal reportedly became unnecessarily leveraged and then needed the parent company's help to insure its survival. Many others have found themselves in this same situation. (It might be noted that in England the U.S. term "highly leveraged" is nonsensical. Rather, they use the phrase "highly geared." These different wordings have confused people on both sides of the Atlantic!)

A U.S. auto manufacturer in Europe encountered problems of a different nature. The company reportedly failed to consider long-run profit margins. As a result, its Spanish division began experiencing a profit squeeze. The managers tried to cut costs by changing labor work loads, sales commission, and even production schedules—all to no avail. In fact, labor resisted and costs actually increased.

Misinterpretations can sometimes cause major financial losses. One company, for example, decided to spend $2 million for a Brazilian plant it seems was not needed. The company's decision to invest the money was based upon an incorrect interpretation of data. The reported sales figures (stated in Brazilian cruzeiros) appeared very promising, but they had not been adjusted for high inflation. Only the number of cruzeiros had grown, not the number of products sold. It is often more prudent to evaluate sales levels employing physical measures (such as weight, volume, number of units, etc.) rather than financial ones. Then inflation and currency value fluctuations are less likely to cause such errors.

Market Research

One of the worst errors a company can make is failing to determine if a market exists for its products or services prior to market entry. Unfortunately, many firms have fallen prey to this mistake and blindly assumed that their products would be desired. At times, they have been "right" (perhaps "lucky" might be the more appropriate word). Other times, however, they have not been so fortunate. Often the market simply was not as promising as anticipated. Several firms have discovered only after initial entry attempts that no market ever existed. Sound and thorough market research would have revealed these and other avoidable problems companies have encountered in international business.

Insufficient market

Companies exporting food products seem to have been especially prone to experiencing difficulty in foreign markets. A U.S. manufacturer of cornflakes, for example, tried to introduce its product in Japan, but the attempt failed miserably. Since the Japanese were not interested in the general concept of breakfast cereals, how could the manufacturer expect them to purchase cornflakes?

A well-known U.S. soft drink company predicted the existence of a large Indonesian market for its product, but the prediction was based on a faulty market research study. The study was conducted in large Indonesian cities and the results were projected to be representative of the entire population. Unfortunately, major differences existed between rural and urban areas of Indonesia. In this case, the cities housed many foreign visitors who purchased the soft drink during the study. When the company concluded that a major market existed, it set up large bottling and distribution facilities but realized only limited sales to city tourists. In conducting market research tests, it is important to determine who is purchasing the product and how representative they are of the entire population.

After learning that ketchup was not available in Japan, a U.S. company is reported to have shipped the Japanese a large quantity of its popular brand-name ketchup. Unfortunately, the firm did not first determine why ketchup was not already marketed in Japan. The large, affluent Japanese market was so tempting that the company feared that any delay would permit its competition to spot the "opportunity" and capture the market. A market test would have revealed the reason behind the lack of availability of ketchup: soy sauce was the preferred condiment there. The company involved, however, was able to purchase Japanese soy sauce for profitable resale in the United States (a possible variation of the old saying, "if you can't beat them, join them").

Kentucky Fried Chicken reportedly found itself in a similar situation when it attempted to enter the Brazilian market. Hoping to eventually open 100 stores, the company began operations in São Paulo. Sales, though, were unexpectedly low. Why? The firm had not thoroughly researched the possible competition. A local variety of low-priced charcoal broiled chicken was available on almost every corner of the city. Because the locals considered this chicken tastier than the Colonel's recipe, Kentucky Fried Chicken hastily revised its plans and began offering hamburgers, Mexican tacos and enchiladas. The company's troubles were not over, however, for these food products were practically unknown in Brazil and met with little customer interest.

Unilever was forced to temporarily withdraw from one of its foreign markets when it learned the hard way that the French were not interested in frozen foods. Happily, the company was able to re-enter the market at a later date offering products more appealing to the French.

CPC International met some resistance when it first tried to sell its dry Knorr soups in the United States. The company had test-marketed the product by serving passersby a small portion of its already prepared warm soup. After the taste test, the individuals were questioned about buying the product. The research revealed U.S. interest, but sales were very low once the packages were placed on grocery store shelves. Further investigation uncovered that the market tests had not taken into account the U.S. tendency to avoid dry soups. During the testing, those individuals interviewed were unaware that they were tasting dried soup. Finding the taste quite acceptable, the interviewees indicated they would be willing to buy the product. Had they known that the soup was sold in a dry form and that the preparation required 15–20 minutes of occasional stirring, they would have shown less interest in the product. In this particular case, the soup's method of preparation was extremely important to the consumer, and the company's failure to test for this unique product difference resulted in a sluggish market.

Clever marketers often analyze product differences and try to use them to the company's advantage. Based on a research study conducted in the United States, one U.S. firm introduced a new cake mix in England. Believing that the housewife would enjoy feeling as if she were participating in the preparation of the cake mix, the U.S. marketers devised the scheme to "add an egg." Thinking they had developed a universal approach, they tried to sell the mix in England. The mix failed, though; the English simply do not like fancy U.S. cakes. They prefer tough and spongy cakes suitable for accompanying their afternoon tea.

Numerous companies have also experienced difficulties when trying to market certain "tasty" products. Tastes desirable to some are often unacceptable to others. Occasionally, a flavor can be successfully modified, but many times it is just totally inappropriate. Warner encountered difficulties when it tried to sell a cinnamon-flavored "Freshen-up" gum in Chile. Because the gum's taste was unacceptable there, the product fared poorly in the marketplace. Coca-Cola also tried to market a product in Chile with little success. When the company attempted to introduce a new grape-flavored drink, it soon discovered that the Chileans were not interested. Apparently, the Chileans prefer wine as their grape drink. These examples exemplify why market research can be so important.

Chase & Sanborn met resistance when it tried to introduce its instant coffee in France. In the French home, the consumption of coffee plays a more significant role than in the English home. Since the preparation of "real" coffee is a touchstone in the life of the French housewife, she will generally reject instant coffee because of its casual characteristics.

A poorly located sales outlet can also contribute to an insufficient market. A classic example involves one of the oldest U.S. fast food companies. This firm, having gained a great deal of domestic experience, decided to open overseas outlets. The management employed sophisticated techniques, and the possible location sites were narrowed down to three addresses in Hamburg, Germany. Careful "traffic counts" were undertaken to determine the best location, and the most frequently passed site was then purchased. A store was built, but sales were surprisingly slow. Was the traffic count in error? No! In this case, while it was true that great numbers of people were passing by the location, hamburgers were not foremost on their minds—they went by the hamburger site only because a major bordello was located next door!

McDonald's also chose an inappropriate location when it first expanded into Europe. The company opened an outlet in a suburb of Amsterdam but soon learned that to attract adequate local traffic, the store should have been downtown. Once the company moved into town, sales immediately improved.

A well-known franchised health club based in New York quickly discovered that what sells in the United States may not sell overseas. Building on its previous success, the firm decided to open a club in Singapore but soon learned that the club did not appeal to the local population. The small expatriate community was delighted with the club, but its numbers were too small to make the club a profitable venture.

Another company tried to market aerosol spray furniture polish in one of the less developed countries. Analysis of the local average income levels suggested that the local population could afford the product. This type of data, though, can be misleading when most of the wealth is concentrated and owned by a few. Therefore, average income levels can erroneously indicate that many people in a population can afford a product. In this particular case, only the few individuals who enjoyed the highest incomes could afford the "luxury" of an aerosol spray furniture polish. Even they, however, were not very interested in the product; they did not believe that such labor saving devices were needed for their servants.

Sometimes the relevant factor determining a product's success involves the technological advancement of the potential customer. A sophisticated product may elicit interest during market testing, but it may fail in the marketplace because it receives a predictably erroneous reputation of undependability. Companies have discovered this fact all too frequently. For example, one company manufactured a product far superior to any similar product being used in a particular African nation. Since market tests indicated strong consumer interest, the firm introduced the product. Shortly thereafter, word spread among the locals that the product was not reliable. This was not true, however. The product broke because the new owners did not understand its maintenance requirements. They refused to oil it even though they were instructed to do so. Because this type of maintenance was atypical of their lifestyle, they soon returned to their earlier, more primitive tools that required no special care. In effect, no market existed for such advanced products.

In some cases, it becomes necessary for a firm to develop a totally new product, one that is completely stripped of frills or complex features. General Motors successfully used this process during the development of its Basic Transportation Vehicle. Singer too profited from its introduction of a basic hand-powered sewing machine.

Although the United States consists of 50 states, the country is usually considered one market. Naturally, subtle cultural differences exist among the states. Neighboring districts in other parts of the world, however, often represent vastly different cultures even though they may be as geographically close as neighboring states. This concept is hard for many U.S. managers to fully understand. The Sunbeam company, for example, assumed that since Germans consumed substantial amounts of toast, the Italians would also. To the company's misfortune, it soon discovered that this did not prove to be the case. The firm encountered additional problems in Italy when it tried to introduce a ladies' electric shaver. Although sales had been fairly strong in some parts of Europe, they remained poor in Italy. Apparently Italian men preferred women with unshaved legs.

People speaking similar languages do not necessarily represent totally similar cultures, either. One U.S. company, assuming that a similar language must indicate similar tastes, tried to sell a U.S. after-shave lotion in England. An expensive advertising campaign was launched but failed. Why? The average British male saw no functional value in the use of after-shave lotion and even believed the use of scents to be effeminate.

Numerous governments have tried to send aid to developing countries. Sometimes, however, their well-intended gifts have been of little use. At one time, for example, great quantities of milk powder were distributed in South America. Claiming that the milk made them ill, the people used it instead to whitewash their houses. Research revealed that the local people were indeed correct. North Americans and Europeans retain an enzyme necessary for the breakdown of milk throughout their lives. Many South Americans, on the other hand, retain the enzyme only while of nursing age. Therefore, the older children and adults were unable to digest the milk. No demand for this product existed even though it was free!

Inadequate feasibility studies

It should now be obvious that a firm needs to conduct research to determine if an adequate market for its products exists. This research must be performed carefully since an inadequate feasibility study may prove more disastrous for the company than none at all.

For instance, one company that chose to cut costs and save time opted to use a feasibility study that a competitor had conducted earlier. At the time the study was originally undertaken, the investment was regarded favorably by the Asian government and the opportunity seemed encouraging. However, the political atmosphere changed during the time that had elapsed. As a result, the firm built its plant but immediately experienced difficulties. The company's use of an outdated feasibility study caused it to overestimate positive results and underestimate probable problems.

Many firms have created headaches for themselves by acting before sufficient data had been gathered. Consider, for example, a well-known U.S. manufacturer of nondurable consumer goods that formed a partnership with a local Japanese company. The Japanese firm supplied encouraging data so, after a one-week investigation by the assistant to the president, the U.S. manufacturer quickly agreed to the arrangement. Not too surprisingly, the venture fell short of expectations. Even with a complete change of top management, the investment stagnated. The company's hasty entry decision had been based upon an inadequate market analysis and the belief that the market would welcome the entry of prestigious U.S. brands. The firm had assumed that it could easily win the confidence of the marketplace and take over a sizable percentage of it.

After a research team verified the existence of an adequate market, one Swiss pharmaceutical firm built an $8 million manufacturing plant in Southeast Asia. The researchers, though, had overlooked an extremely important feature of the market—the local black market. Because of this added competition, the firm experienced lower earnings than expected and found itself with excess production capacity.

Sometimes what appears to be a thorough feasibility study simply is not. After conducting what was believed to be an intensive study, one firm discovered that a number of factors that should have been considered prior to its entrance abroad had been overlooked. Initial research confirmed the desirability of erecting an iron and steel mill, but the mill was forced to close its doors within one year. All equipment was removed and the building was stripped. Those involved in the feasibility study had correctly determined the availability of labor. They had failed, however, to report that the country under consideration was one in which private ownership was inconsistent with the policies of social reform supported by the government. Almost all manufacturing was publicly owned and operated. The laborers, many of whom had been exploited on farms, were encouraged to believe in "capitalistic exploitation." Consequently, they constantly demanded higher wages and increased benefits. Labor unrest, low output, and poor quality resulted. The feasibility study should have revealed the existence of this popular "public ownership" ideology. Since another firm had failed earlier in a similar investment for similar reasons, the investors should have been tipped off that a recurrence of the problem was likely.

As a final example, consider the experience of the Rheem company in the Italian market. The firm's initial strategy of buying raw materials from a local firm, ISI, also included selling the finished product, welded pipe, locally. The plan was put into operation, but Rheem soon learned that not only did ISI produce the same welded pipe, it also maintained insider contracts with the major buyer of the pipe—the government. Because Rheem was buying its raw material from ISI, it was unable to undercut ISI's price and, as a foreign-owned firm, it was not able to secure the Italian government contracts. Unfortunately, it had not developed any export plans. Thorough research should have uncovered these problems and thus Rheem would have known to consider alternative plans.

As evidenced, a firm's reliance on outdated or incomplete feasibility studies can cause it to blunder. Improperly conducted studies can also create difficulties. This is easily illustrated by a classic story that involves the market research conducted some years ago by *Reader's Digest*. The researchers concluded from their findings that the Germans and the French consumed more spaghetti than Italians. Further analysis revealed that this false finding surfaced as a result of the questions asked. The survey questions dealt with the purchases of branded and packaged spaghetti. Many Italians, however, buy spaghetti in bulk. By qualifying the way in which the product was purchased, the researchers arrived at a false conclusion about spaghetti consumption. To conduct sound market research, one must pay strict attention to both method and content.

SUMMARY

This chapter has focused on the importance of paying attention to detail. Seemingly minor points of law can create major problems for companies. Financial strategies, market research, and feasibility studies must all be undertaken and conducted with great care. In fact, the significance of meticulous research has been stressed throughout this book.

CHAPTER 9

Lessons Learned

- Adaptation
- Nationalism
- Promotion
- Translation
- Market Research
- Conclusion

Lessons Learned

As discussed in the previous chapters, international businesses can indeed encounter a variety of unexpected developments. Occasionally, some of these surprises benefit the companies involved. Unfortunately, in numerous other instances, the surprises prove to be undesirable and often costly. Many of the troubles encountered by firms in the past actually could have been avoided.

Venturing overseas can be extremely tricky. A company may employ sophisticated management techniques but still blunder if any detail is overlooked. Even failing to ask the right question can cause a blunder. Unfortunately, there are hundreds of reported cases of companies blundering overseas. These errors are indeed regrettable, but we can learn from them. There is no need to repeat the mistakes others have made.

Adaptation

Numerous headaches have resulted when firms have failed to correctly adapt their products or packages to local environments. Sometimes it is only the color of the package that needs to be altered to enhance a product's sales. Since color preferences and symbols vary from country to country, it is wise to seek local advice as locals are aware of such "bad" colors.

A lesser-known variable worthy of consideration is "number." Packages that prominently display a specific number increase the risk of consumer avoidance. Since many people believe in lucky and unlucky numbers, even the number of products pictured on a label can prove troublesome.

Sometimes it is neither the number displayed on the package nor the color that creates a problem, but rather the picture on the label. In many other instances the product itself requires alteration. Food, beverages, and tobacco products often need to be modified in order to accommodate the tastes of local consumers. Cigarette manufacturers learned long ago that U.S. brands sell well overseas—if the tobacco is carefully blended to suit local preferences. Products that are not modified to meet local needs, of course, face a high risk of failing in the marketplace.

Sometimes the company or product name may require modification. A domestically successful name may be inappropriate or ineffective in a foreign market. Names have created many a humorous, obscene, offensive or unexpected situation.

Nationalism

Many avoidable problems have occurred because managers have been insensitive to the nationalistic feelings of the natives of the host country. It is usually best for companies to maintain low profiles in overseas ventures. There is seldom any need for a firm to try to turn an overseas manufacturing plant into an exact duplicate of its home plant. Companies that have tried to do this have often met stiff resistance from both employees and local customers.

Foreign manufacturers in the United States learned this lesson long ago. Many U.S. laborers are now working for foreign-owned firms but are unaware of their company's origins. Managers should avoid any unnecessary comparisons that might reflect the home country management's belief that the host country might be inferior in some way to the home country. It is often possible—sometimes even desirable—to compare products, but it is not prudent to publicly compare governments, labor, or technology.

It may be wise to hire most, if not all, top-level managers of the foreign subsidiary from the available host country management pool. Not only will these individuals project a more local image, but also they usually understand local problems well and can often help the company avoid blunders.

If an expatriate is to be hired, extra care must be taken. Effective expatriate managers must possess special abilities and traits if they are to avoid blundering. Among the most important characteristics are:

- An ability to get along well with people.
- An awareness of cultural differences.
- Open mindedness.
- Tolerance of foreign cultures.
- Adaptability to new cultures, ideas, and challenges.
- An ability to adjust quickly to new conditions.
- An interest in facts, not blind assumptions.
- Previous business experience.
- Previous experience with foreign cultures.
- An ability to learn foreign languages.

Promotion

Many companies have encountered serious problems trying to coordinate their sales efforts. All plans should be in writing, and it is advisable to charge someone with the responsibility of central coordination. Thus, risks are lessened and money-saving opportunities may arise. Coca-Cola, for instance, requires that all overseas marketing plans be submitted to the central office well before they are instituted. This allows the company time to examine the concepts. The firm's experience with similar plans can be reviewed and necessary changes can be made. Sometimes central company managers discover that similar plans have failed in other overseas ventures or sometimes they determine that similar plans have succeeded. There is no need to reinvent the wheel. Coordination not only reduces the possibility of errors, it also provides a company with the opportunity to fine-tune its promotions.

Another company well known for its successful marketing campaigns is Anheuser-Busch. It uses some of the same themes in many countries (its ants ads were especially popular in China) and ties in with major sports events around the world, but only after careful evaluation of each market. As Steve Burrows, President and CEO of Anheuser-Busch International reports, most marketing initiatives are modified to fit the local markets.

Dozens of blunders have been made by firms that failed to carefully investigate the local customs and preferences of their potential customers. Since social norms vary so greatly from country to country, it is extremely difficult for any outsider to be knowledgeable of them all. As pointed out previously, local input can be vital. Many promotional errors could have been averted had this warning been heeded.

Translation

Advertising is a tricky business. More mistakes seem to have been made in advertising than in any other business task, and these errors have most often been caused by faulty translations. It is usually recommended that the translation of an advertisement stress the ad's general theme and concept rather than precisely duplicate the original slogan.

There are several methods known which can help a company avert potential translation disasters. Certainly a company may hire an exceptionally brilliant translator, but certain types of errors can still surface. The translator may enjoy an extraordinary gift for the language or have studied in the foreign country but may be unfamiliar with many idiomatic expressions and slang. Therefore, in many cases it is wise to also hire a second translator, one familiar with the local slang and unusual idioms, to "backtranslate."

Backtranslation is one of the best techniques available to reduce translation errors. Backtranslation requires that one individual translate the message into the desired foreign language and that another party translate the foreign version "back" into the original language. Thus, a company can determine if its intended message is actually being presented. An Australian soft drink company discovered the value of backtranslation during the planning stages of its entry into the Hong Kong market. The company had hoped to employ its successful slogan "Baby, it's cold inside," but before using the translated version of the slogan, the firm had it translated back into English. This proved to be a wise move. The message backtranslated to "Small mosquito, on the inside it is very cold." "Small mosquito," a local colloquial expression for a small child, simply did not convey the same thing as the friendly English slang word "baby" for "woman." The intended message would have been lost had the original translated version been used.

The use of backtranslation uncovers many translation errors but can be frustrating if performed by mediocre translators. Naturally, the better the translator is, the fewer the problems encountered. The difficulty, therefore, lies in determining the ability of a potential translator. One slow and expensive method is to allow the translator a trial run. This method will expose any problems, but it then becomes necessary to determine if the errors were committed by the original translator or by the person translating back to the first language.

Firms requiring major or important translation work should thoroughly investigate any potential translator. The following points should be covered during the candidate's interview.

- Does the translator maintain or have access to a library or reference books dealing with the appropriate subject and industry?
- Does the translator understand the required technical terms? Does the translator know the foreign words for these specialized terms? If not, how are they to be learned? Does the translator have a staff or access to experts in various fields (e.g., law)?
- Will someone check the work? If so, what are the credentials of the assistant? (It is often advisable to request references and copies of material translated for other clients.)
- How recently has the translator been to the country involved? (Sometimes it is necessary to determine how current the translator's knowledge is. Because languages do change (especially slang), it is not enough to hire someone familiar with the foreign language and culture. Even a native tends to lose track of slang and idioms after being away from home for a few years.)

Once a translator has been chosen, there are several things that a company can do to facilitate the job. For instance, since it has often taken the company many months to develop the promotional materials, a translator should not be asked to translate the material hurriedly. Given adequate time, a much better translation is likely to result. A simple literal translation is not generally appropriate, so a translator may need time to be creative.

Of course, this is not to say that the translator should not be given a deadline. It is important to tell the person when the material must be finished and the timing of its expected use. On occasion, a manager has failed to inform the translator of the season in which the ad is to run, and the translator has assumed an inappropriate time period. A company does little to enhance its image when it runs a winter advertisement in the summer. (A few companies have also blundered by promoting advertisements during ill-suited seasons when they simply forgot that the southern hemisphere has the opposite seasons of the northern hemisphere.)

Naturally, it is important for the translator to understand the type of media to be used and the general characteristics of the audience. This allows the person to determine the proper level of formality and the correct tone. A translator must be given the freedom to modify original wording. As discussed previously, literal translations can prove disastrous.

Also, because the translated version of a message may require more words than the original, it is not wise to limit the translator to a particular amount of time or space. Doing so may seriously jeopardize the effectiveness of the message.

If possible, firms are advised to reduce the use of overly technical terms and to avoid industry jargon in their promotional materials. It is also advisable to limit the use of large numbers. Any number over 10,000 may be easily mistranslated. The number "billion," for example, is numerically written with nine zeroes in the United States but with 12 zeroes in Europe.

Since humor is also almost impossible to translate, it is best to avoid using jokes in advertising. What is regarded as funny by some is often not considered so by others.

Finally, a translator should be provided with as much relevant information as possible and should be informed of the message's objectives and what is essential to the theme. By allowing the translator to examine previous company translations as well as translated slogans of competing companies, the individual can not only assure that any key phrase associated with the company is included but can avoid accidentally using any competitors' phrases.

To reduce translation needs and overcome communication difficulties in countries that experience high levels of illiteracy, visual methods of communication are sometimes used. Libby, for instance, has successfully promoted its products through inexpensive commercials that feature a clown enjoying Libby products. In these ads, no words are spoken.

Using English in non-English-speaking countries

Sometimes companies have found that the best solution to the translation problem is simply to not translate the material. If the locals can understand English, or if they simply do not need to comprehend the message, then it may be safer for a firm from an English-speaking country to stick with its English copy. The use of translators is always risky, because they are putting words into the company's mouth. A firm does not need them to put a foot in there also!

To reduce the problems which may occur when English is used in a non-English-speaking country:

- Keep the entire message short and simple, including words and sentences.
- Avoid jargon or slang.
- Avoid idioms.
- Avoid humor if possible.
- Use appropriate currencies and measurements.
- Cite examples if feasible.
- Repeat important points.

If a company decides to go ahead with an English message through a verbal advertisement directed to an audience whose native language is not English, the speaker should speak slowly, carefully and correctly pronounce all words, pausing between sentences.

As it is very likely that during some part of the overseas planning or management someone from the company will engage in a conversation with an individual who has some difficulty understanding English, the following guidelines should be followed:

- Time should be allowed for questions and discussions.
- Patience is important—permit the individual to find the words to respond.
- Questions should be asked to determine if the message has been comprehended.
- The individual should be complimented and reassured of his or her ability to speak English.
- Express gratefulness that the individual is speaking English.
- Express regret that the conversation could not have been spoken in the other person's language. (It should be noted, however, that a few polite social words spoken in the foreign language are appreciated and highly recommended.)

Ideally, company literature and material should be provided prior to the conversation. This allows the other individual a chance to prepare and should greatly increase the person's comprehension. After the discussion, the person should be sent a summary of the conversation. This also will increase the likelihood that the conversation was correctly understood.

During World War II, the phrase "loose lips sink ships" was used to discourage people from talking about military matters when they were within the hearing range of strangers. For international businesses the phrase might be appropriately modified to "misunderstood lips sink companies." Multinational firms will encounter enough unavoidable and unpredictable problems to be tried and tested. They need not make avoidable blunders as well.

Market Research

The use of properly conducted market research could have reduced or eliminated most international business blunders. Market researchers have the ability to uncover adaptation needs, potential name problems, promotional requirements, and proper market strategies. Even many of the translation blunders could have been avoided if sound research techniques had been used.

A number of the cited blunders occurred because firms tried to use the same product, name, promotional material or strategy overseas that they used at home. They were hoping that what worked well at home would also work well abroad. Although this is understandable, it is nevertheless often unrealistic. Although standardization promotes certain efficiencies, in many instances it is not a worthwhile strategy to pursue. Limitations do exist, and it is important for firms to recognize and understand this.

The use of market research enables a firm to determine its limits of standardization. The research serves two major functions: it can help a company identify what the firm can hope to accomplish and it can help a company realize what the firm should not do. Neither dimension should be overlooked.

This might best be illustrated with the experience of one European vehicle manufacturer. It tried to sell its standard line of trucks in Saudi Arabia, but sales were far below expectations. After several frustrating years, it conducted market research to understand the problems. The results were a shock. Not only did it firmly establish that the Saudi drivers had a strong brand loyalty for a competitor's product, the research also revealed that the Saudis did not like the flat-front style of the trucks being offered (preferring the more rounded front on competing trucks), the larger service facilities introduced (seeming too impersonal and inflexible), and even the size of the truck's front seat (too small). It turns out, Saudi drivers typically carry many passengers in their trucks and did not want to change their habits.

Few would question the value of marketing research as part of international business planning. Unfortunately, it is not an easy undertaking and is extremely complicated. Even the smallest of details must not be ignored during analysis. The data required varies with the firm, its products, and the decisions being made. Research helps a company determine whether or not to go abroad, which countries to enter, how to enter the foreign markets, and which marketing strategies to use.

Conclusion

This collection of international business blunders was not gathered with the intention of using it to poke fun at multinational companies or to make them appear inept. Rather, it was assembled to provide valuable, vicarious examples of business practices that should be avoided. The blunders others have experienced provide us with interesting lessons—ones surely preferable to learning through experience.

In reality, companies are generally quite competent. Considering the many ways a firm can blunder, it must be doing most things correctly just to survive. This thought was best expressed by a senior executive from General Motors when he was asked to verify one of the problems reported in this book. He replied that although GM may have made a few errors overseas, when that very small number is compared with the many decisions made by GM, it is "a good batting average." This is true. Most firms make few serious mistakes and even fewer avoidable blunders. If they did make many blunders, they simply would not be in business long. Although numerous errors have been committed, one must realize that the mistakes have been made by many different companies over a number of years.

The fact that firms make these mistakes should not be all that surprising anyway. After all, it is not really a company that blunders, but its employees. Employees are only human, and we all make mistakes. Sometimes our errors are personal, but sometimes they are made on behalf of corporations.

It should also be noted that the blunders reported may not be totally accurate. Although most of the anecdotes have been reported in the media and efforts were made to verify them, verification has not been easy. Many corporations have been reluctant to respond to inquiries. Several firms have replied with a version of "we are sorry but we cannot provide you with the information about that possible event. The person who had been responsible for that area is *no longer with the company.*" These statements possibly bear an added message: if one wants to remain with a firm, avoid making blunders.

Since firms do not appreciate appearing foolish, they sometimes deny a witnessed event. But as the public becomes more and more aware that all firms have made some mistakes, these denials become less necessary. There are cases, however, where reports of company blunders have proven to be false. The wrong companies have been identified or the entire story has been fictionalized. This author discovered an excellent example of a false report when trying to verify a story regarding Exxon's ventures in Thailand. The report stated that Exxon's ad "Put a tiger in your tank" failed in Thailand because the tiger does not represent power and strength there. However, a series of letters and investigations in both Asia and the United States revealed what had really happened. Overzealous competitors had deliberately planted the false story, hoping the U.S. media would pick it up. In fact, not only is the tiger a symbol of strength in Thailand, Exxon continued to use the ad effectively and was able to capture a large share of the local market.

Unfortunately, this book may also contain a few errors. Naturally, any error is greatly regretted. There certainly have been errors of omission, as this book does not cite or report every blunder ever committed.

One final word of warning: no one should be under the illusion that all blunders have been committed; others are likely to occur. The more we learn of past blunders, the more we will understand them and their causes and the better we can prepare ourselves to avoid future blunders. Hopefully, this book will help reduce the number of blunders made. We do not want your future decisions to end up being reported in the next edition of this book!

Notes

1 Introduction

1 More information on this and similar incidents is reported by Edward T. Hall in *The Silent Language* (New York: Doubleday, 1959).
2 A 32-page booklet, *International Business Gift-giving Customs* by Kathleen Reardon, deals with the problems of international gift giving. It is published by the Parker Pen Company, PO Box 5100, Janesville, Wisconsin, 53547.

2 Production

1 Many versions of this event exist. Most historians, however, currently seem to believe that the bullets encased in pig wax represented the "final straw." Basically, the bullets provided an example of the degree of British insensitivity to Indian cultural values and needs. In reality, the East India Company needed to modify its entire operation.

3 Names

1 For further details see Carolyn Pfaff, "Champagne Cigs Cause Headache," *Advertising Age*, March 30, 1981, p. 2.

5 Translation

1 Although many people have cited the "pregnancy" problem experienced by Parker Pen, they seldom provide any details. The author, therefore, thanks the Parker Pen Company management for its open and refreshingly frank discussion of this past event and what caused it. All firms have at one time or another made mistakes. If more firms would be as helpful as the Parker Pen Company, then we could all more clearly understand the underlying causes of these errors and avoid them in the future.

2 This list was adapted from Maurice Brisebois, "Industrial Advertising and Marketing in Quebec," *The Marketer*, spring–summer 1966, p. 10.

7 Strategic Management

1 "Golden Touches Turned to Lead," *Time*, November 30, 1981, p. 66.

8 Other Areas of International Business

1 The complaint, voiced by Colgate-Palmolive, dealt with the possibility of consumers mistaking the two products. Although many firms face competition from counterfeit products, Unilever argued that it was not attempting any such strategy. However, Australian courts ruled that the resemblance was too great. For details read Len Blanket, "Aussi Court Bans Package Ad," *Advertising Age*, October 12, 1981, p. 72.

Index of Companies

Index of Places

Index of Products